I0483420

HOW TO GET INTO AND SURVIVE FILM, ADVERTISING AND TV POST-PRODUCTION.
THE ALTERNATIVE GUIDE.

Klaudija Cermak

HOW TO GET INTO AND SURVIVE FILM, ADVERTISING AND TV POST-PRODUCTION.
THE ALTERNATIVE GUIDE.

Klaudija Cermak

Editor: Charlie Wilson

Book Design: John Amy

Cover design: Rosa Lykiardopoulos

ISBN 978-0-9572170-3-4

Dedication

To Ted, without whom I would have nothing to write. To Majda, who always encouraged me to write. To Ivana, who told me what not to write.

Contents

Introduction

THIS book answers all the questions that students asked me following my master classes on post-production over the last few years at London universities.

When I started working in the industry in the mid '80s, post-production as we know it today was in its infancy and jobs were plentiful.

There was scope for great creativity, often driven by the very high standards set by BBC. As an artist one had great freedom to express oneself through, and while experimenting with, new technologies. One was also able to navigate through different parts of the post-production industry and forge a career across TV, advertising and film.

Today the roles are much more defined and specialised and artists rarely cross from one part of the industry to another. That's why it's more important than ever to choose one's career path with care and keep focused on achieving one's ultimate dream.

The work
www.klaudijacermak.com

The blog
www.survivingpostproduction.wordpress.com
Look forward to meeting you there!

PRONOUN DISCLAIMER
Please note that I am using male pronouns rather than gender-neutral pronouns throughout the book for the simplicity of writing.

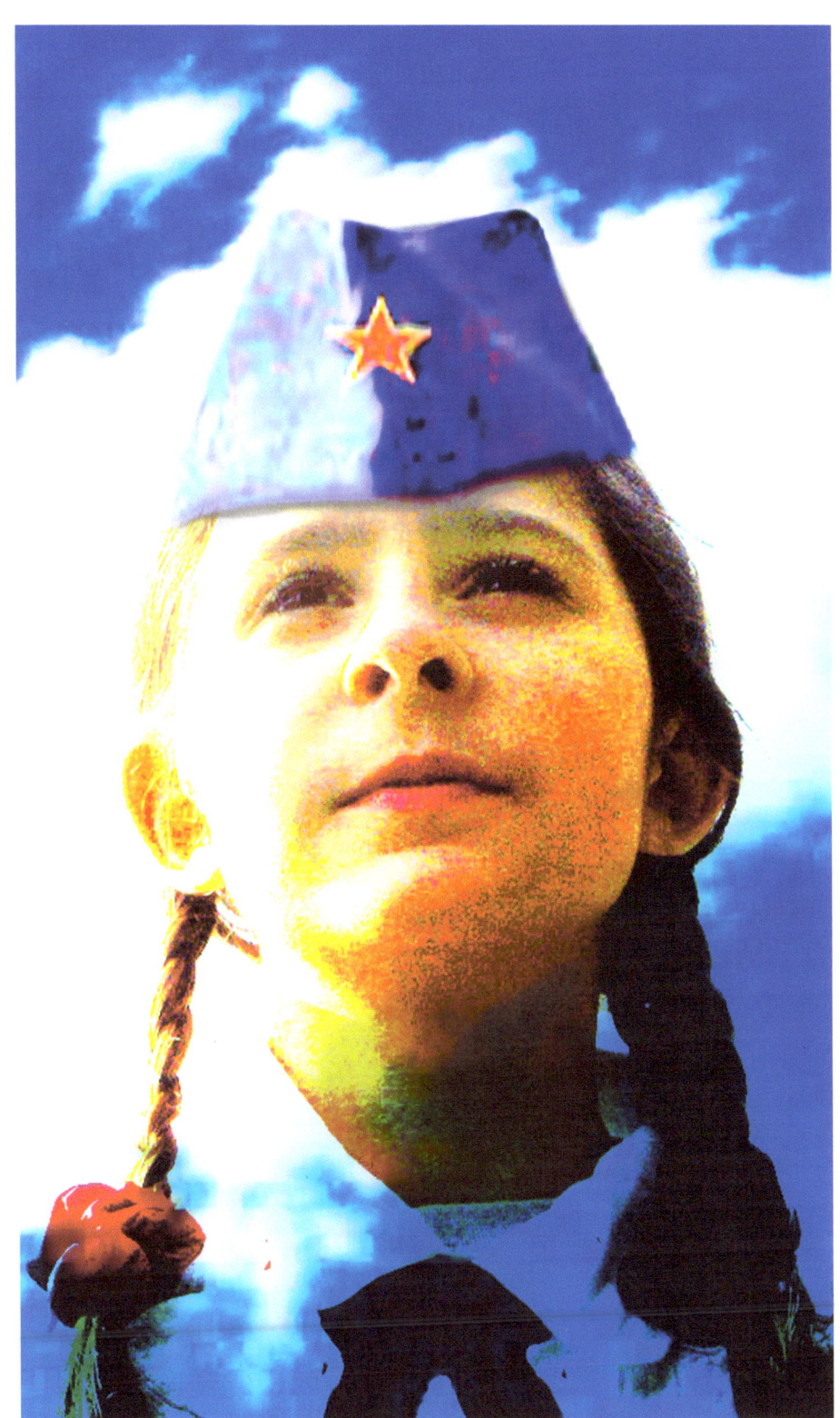

"When I grow up I'm going to be"

I grew up in the Socialist Federative Republic of Yugoslavia, so the first thing I ever wanted to be was a Pioneer.

Over the years what I wanted to be changed many times, usually driven by films I watched or books I read, but it had always involved being a goodie or a hero.

Only a few people are lucky enough to know what they wish to be when they grow up – even when they are grown up.

Nowadays, one's whole life is defined by the work one does and most of one's time is likely to be spent at work too.

So the sooner you decide who you wish to be, the easier it is, and the further you will get. Start making a list now!

Ben Hur, Winnetou, Cinderella,
Gandhi, Nada, Julia,
an actress, ballet
dancer, heart surgeon,
Mayakovski, Mother
Theresa, a singer,
a pianist, Bob Dylan,
James Bond, an artist,
a director, Bertolt
Brecht, Simon Wiesenthal,
Peter Ustinov, a lawyer,
Edward Said, a journalist,
an editor, a producer,
an artist.

"I'm an artist"

Then the first thing you should consider doing is joining the art world.

It is open to new ideas.

It allows you to create original and challenging work.

It lets you question and have an impact on the world around you.

And, most importantly, it has no clients!

Having a client means sitting on the corridor floor crying, as he has asked you to replicate something you created for another job.

Or, even worse, he has asked you to replicate something that someone else has created for another job.

However tempting a list of post-production jobs may be, very few have any creative control – and the ultimate control belongs to the man in a suit holding the wallet.

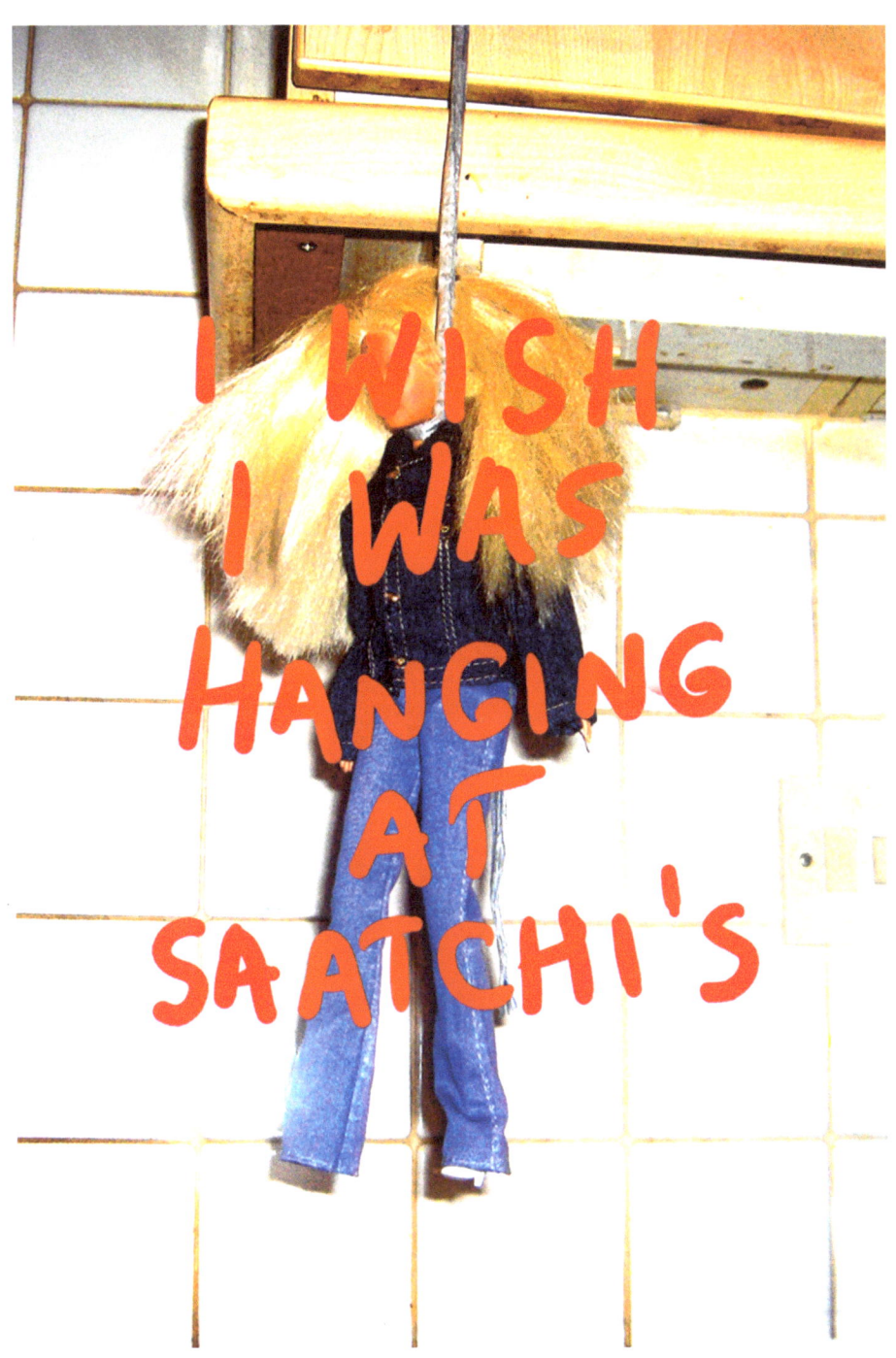

I WISH I WAS HANGING AT SAATCHI'S

"But I love moving images"

Loving moving images isn't enough.

In post-production, you have to be willing to sit in front of the computer in complete darkness from 9 to 6 (if you are lucky), five days a week (at least), for the rest of your life (if you are really lucky). Not alone, but with dozens of people around you sitting still, staring at their screens and listening to their music, sometimes with no one to talk to.

Or you have to be prepared to sit still, staring at the screen with no music to listen to, with a dozen people sitting behind you, scrutinising everything you do. Just imagine having to concentrate on adding a pip to a sliced pear (on the computer), while at the same time entertaining and comforting everyone around you.

So, be realistic! If you prefer open fields to closed spaces, or animals to people, this is not going to work.

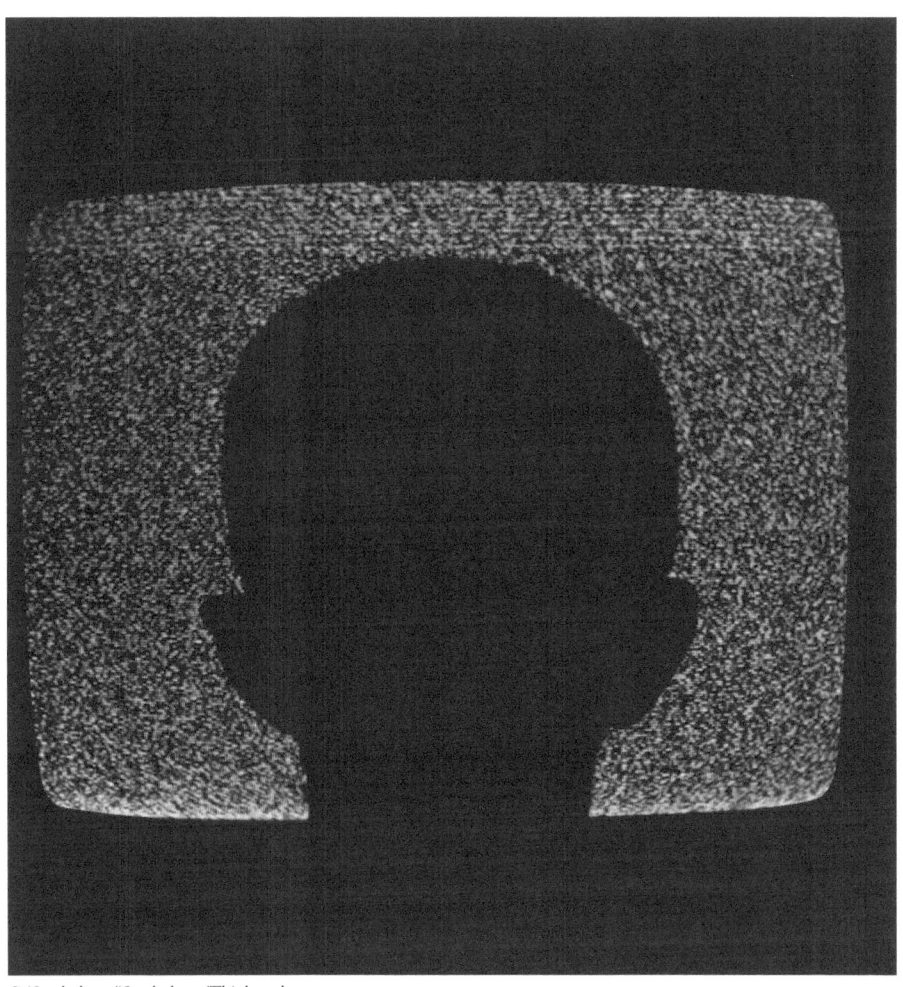

Creating a moving image

The process of creating a moving image is always the same, just on a different scale. After all these stages, they are distributed to cinemas or go on air, either on TV or the Web.

DEVELOPMENT

↓

PREPRODUCTION

↓

PRODUCTION

↓

POST-PRODUCTION

In a nutshell

Development

An idea, a book or a story is developed into the script and the money is raised.

Pre-production

Cast and crew are hired. Locations are found. Sets are built and costumes are made.

Production

The shoot.

Post-production

The footage is sent to the lab to be developed (if it has been shot on film). It is then transferred to video or to digital disk, graded and edited. Animation, visual effects, graphics, titles and audio are added. The rule of thumb is that the longer you spend in pre-production, the smoother production is and the more efficient the time spent in post-production is.

The magic of post-production

Post-production is where the moving images take shape and the story is told. It is the most exhilarating environment, full of creative, talented and quirky individuals, working together to create a story that will entertain or enlighten you – or just make you shop till you drop.

This is where elements from the shoot are cut, assembled and seamlessly combined with the elements created in post-production through editing, grading, visual effects, motion graphics and sound.

Sometimes the landscapes are extended, the super-humans made, the disasters created, the creatures built, the armies formed, the dead awoken, the heads replaced, the aliens born and the brands polished.

In post-production, anything is possible – if you have money or time or, preferably, both.

"We'll fix it in post"

This is one of the most common phrases on the shoot, and it's true.
Almost everything can be fixed in post-production, besides the script and the
acting – if one has the money or the time (and often one has neither).
However, after a re-shoot has been considered, they are somehow both found,
because re-shooting is even more expensive – and losing the client is out of the
question.

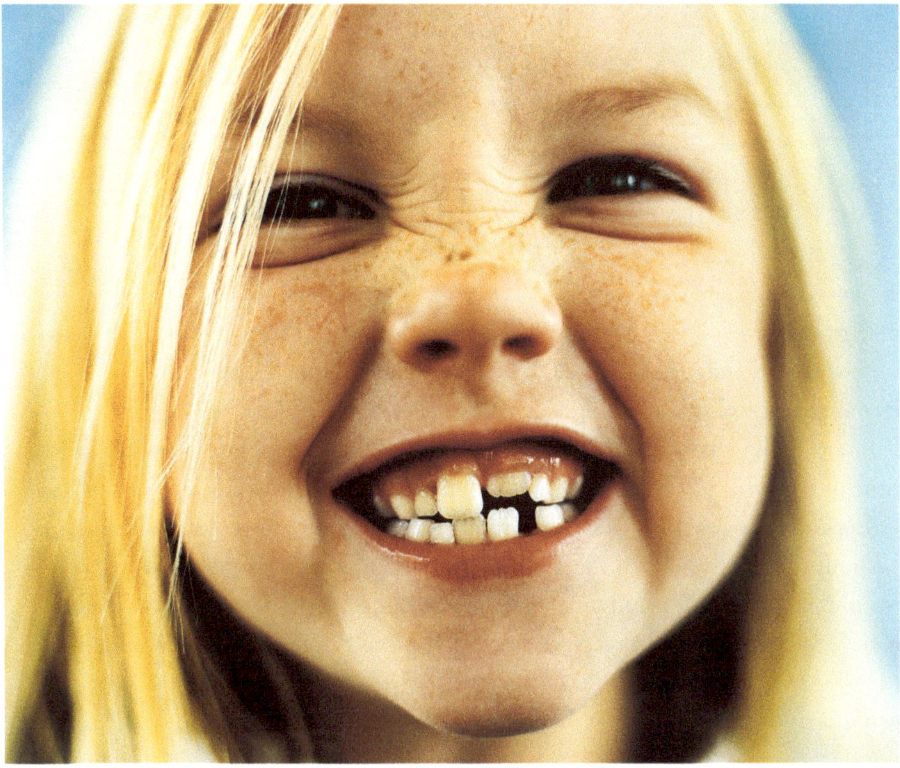

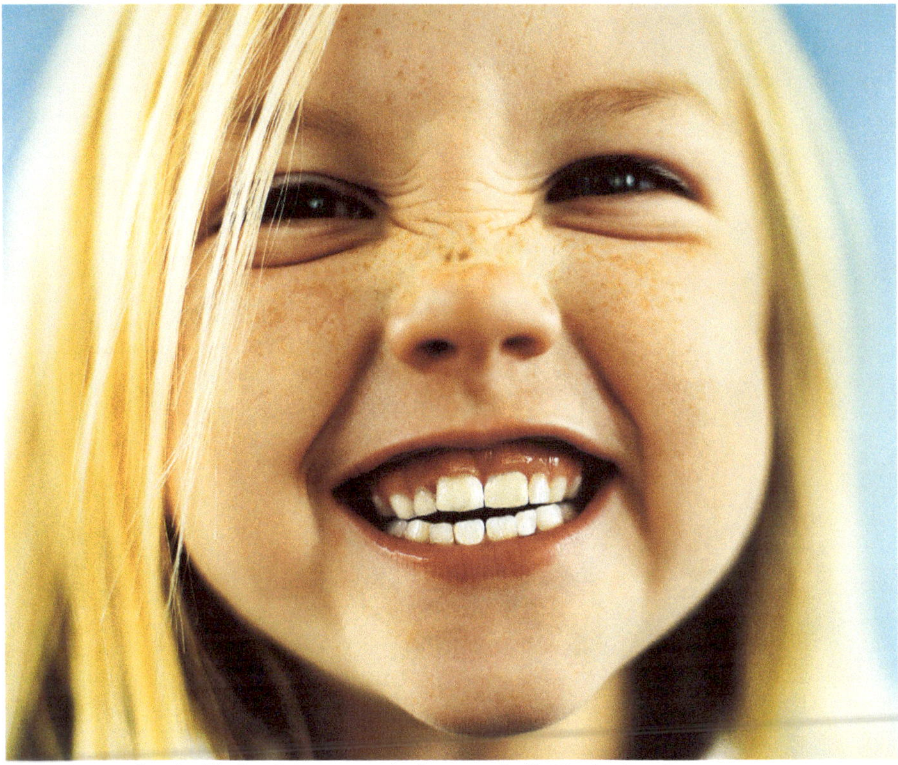

© Digital Vision/Photodisc/Thinkstock. Bottom mage has been retouched by Klaudija Cermak.

"I would do anything to get to do that"

Then you can start as a runner.

The runner's role hasn't been invented to exploit you or to torture you; it is there to test your character and your hunger to get into the industry.

If you play it right, you are in.

Runners are in charge of hospitality, ensuring the clients' comfort during their time in the facility. They bring regular refreshments to both the clients and the artists and do whatever is necessary to ease the smooth completion of the job, without the disruptions of the real world. This may range from picking up people's dry cleaning or buying a present for someone to doing local deliveries. Runners also do menial tasks like stocking up the fridges, moving boxes and occasionally cleaning the toilets after everyone's great Friday night out.

Just close your eyes and keep thinking of your ultimate goal!

"But I don't want to clean the toilets!"

This is the wrong attitude, but okay, you may be lucky, or unlucky, and skip the runner's part.

Either you or your family knows someone or knows someone who knows someone in the industry, who may get you in as a junior.

It has happened before.

Or there could be a sudden technological development, resulting in a recruitment drive to fill a number of positions requiring a particular skill, for which the companies are willing to train you, if you already have the basic skills and the talent. This has recently happened with stereoscopic film conversions, causing a sudden demand for stereoscopic rotoscope and compositing artists. Some compositing courses' students were offered the jobs with additional training from companies that experienced a sudden deluge in film stereo conversions work.

So keep an eye on family friends and new developments in the area you want to get into.

Learn to make a nice hot cup of tea

When I arrived in London, I was armed with a variety of skills but apart from a
long list of politically incorrect jokes, few were relevant to survival in the virtual
world. Being able to shoot pretty well from an M48 Mauser or knowing the
words of all the revolutionary songs from Spain to the Soviet Union were fun,
but not very useful. But the jokes were.

Marx, Engels and Lenin are discussing if it's better to have a wife or a lover. Marx
says, 'A wife, she looks after you so you have plenty of time to study'. Engels says,
'It's better to have a lover, you can see her whenever you wish so you can study
any time you want'. Lenin shakes his head and says, 'The best is to have both.
The wife thinks you are with the lover, the lover thinks you are with the wife and
you can go to the library and study, study and study.'

The first thing you need to study is how to make a nice hot cup of tea.

This is the one skill that can make a real difference to your career.

1. Fill the kettle with fresh water.

2. Boil the water.

3. Place one tea bag per cup of water in the teapot.

4. Pour the boiling water into the teapot.

5. Cover the teapot and let the tea brew for five minutes.

6. Pour the tea into a cup.

7. Add a bit of milk.

8. Place a biscuit in the saucer.

9. Place a bowl of sugar on the tray.

10. Serve.

One thing to beware of is if your tea is too good, it may take you longer to move
up the ladder within the company.

Good tea-makers are hard to find.

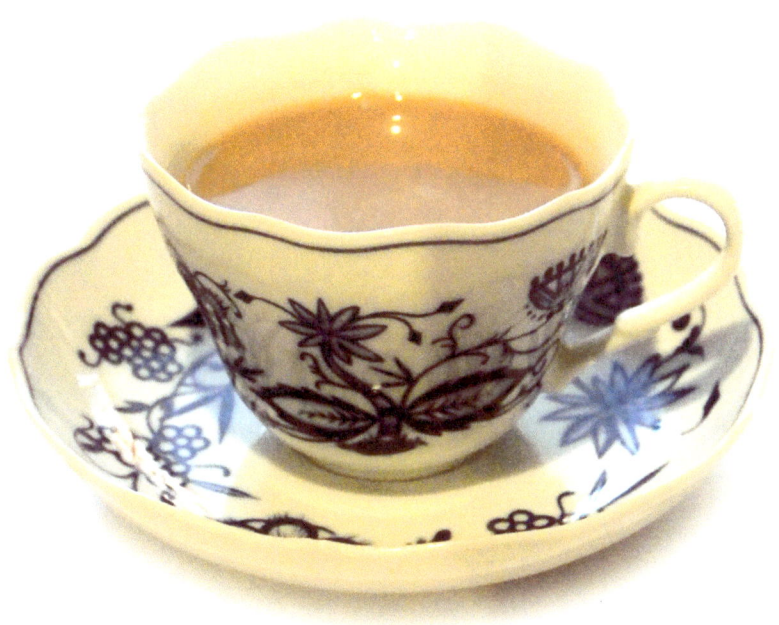

GETTING IN

The lucky way

My career in post-production started by stepping on someone's foot at a party.
It was unintentional, but it got me talking to a nice young man.
A few sentences later, I was in love.
A few days later, I was introduced to his friends – a bunch of scientists who ran a company making visual effects equipment.
A few months later, I was given the keys to their offices and let loose on their computers.
Being in the right place at the right time can put a stop to the endless dilemmas of what you are going to be when you grow up.
P.S. Don't step on people's feet too hard.

The traditional way

The traditional way of getting a job in post-production is to start as a runner and build your way to the top.

It requires tons of enthusiasm and the willingness to work very long hours for peanuts.

But first you have to become one.

With dozens of applications dropping onto the recruitment desks every day, yours has to stand out.

One runner sent a worn out, battered trainer with his CV.

He got the job.

The advantages of being a runner are that you meet a lot of people working in the industry, you get an insight into the workings of the company and you have time to assess which role you may want to pursue.

You are able to ask questions and meet people doing the job you may want to do and you get the opportunity to play around on the equipment in downtime.

The free way

Landing an internship or work experience is another way of getting your foot in the door.

Basically, you offer to work for free.

If you can't afford to work for free, combine this with a paid job.

An internship gives you an opportunity to experience first-hand what you are trying to get yourself into, and it may change or re-enforce your career aspirations.

Be helpful, chat to others and pick up as many tips as possible on how to stay in.

Show passion when making tea and doing photocopies.

Take people out for drink after work.

This may be your first step in building the invaluable network of people for your future career.

Enthusiasm and willingness can take you a long way.

P.S. You should not work for longer than four weeks on no pay.

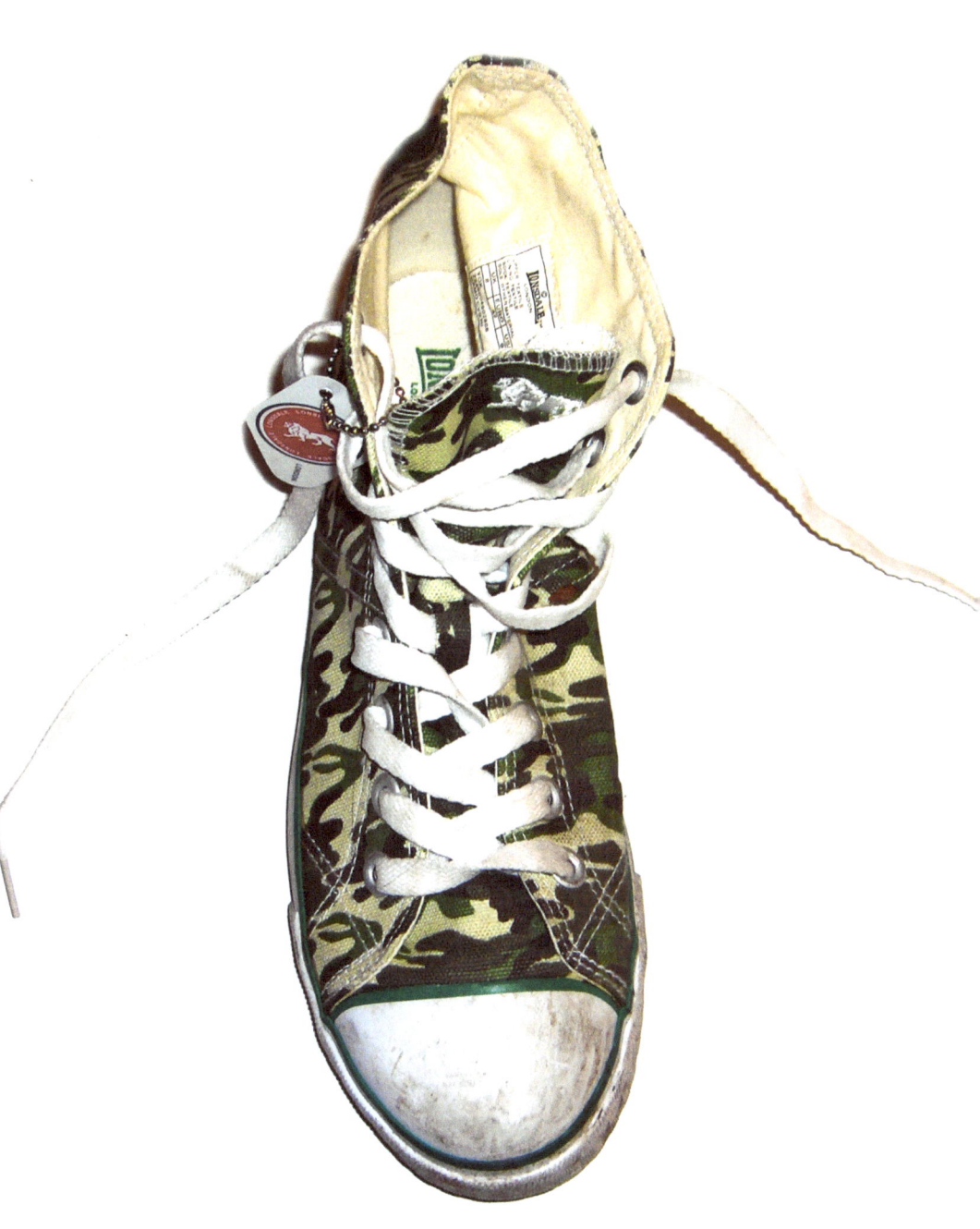

The smart way

1. Choose a course that will give you the theoretical grounding as well as the practical one.

2. Spend your free time mastering the key software used in the area of post-production you are interested in.

3. Check out showreels of people doing the job you want to do.

4. Plan and create work for your showreel. The sort of work that will get you noticed.

5. Offer your services for free on interesting projects that you can add to your showreel and to your CV.

6. Send out the showreel, filled with great work and polished to a high standard, to TV production companies.

7. Pitch for work against the heavyweights.

P.S. If it doesn't work out, you can always apply to work as a runner. Never give up on your dreams!

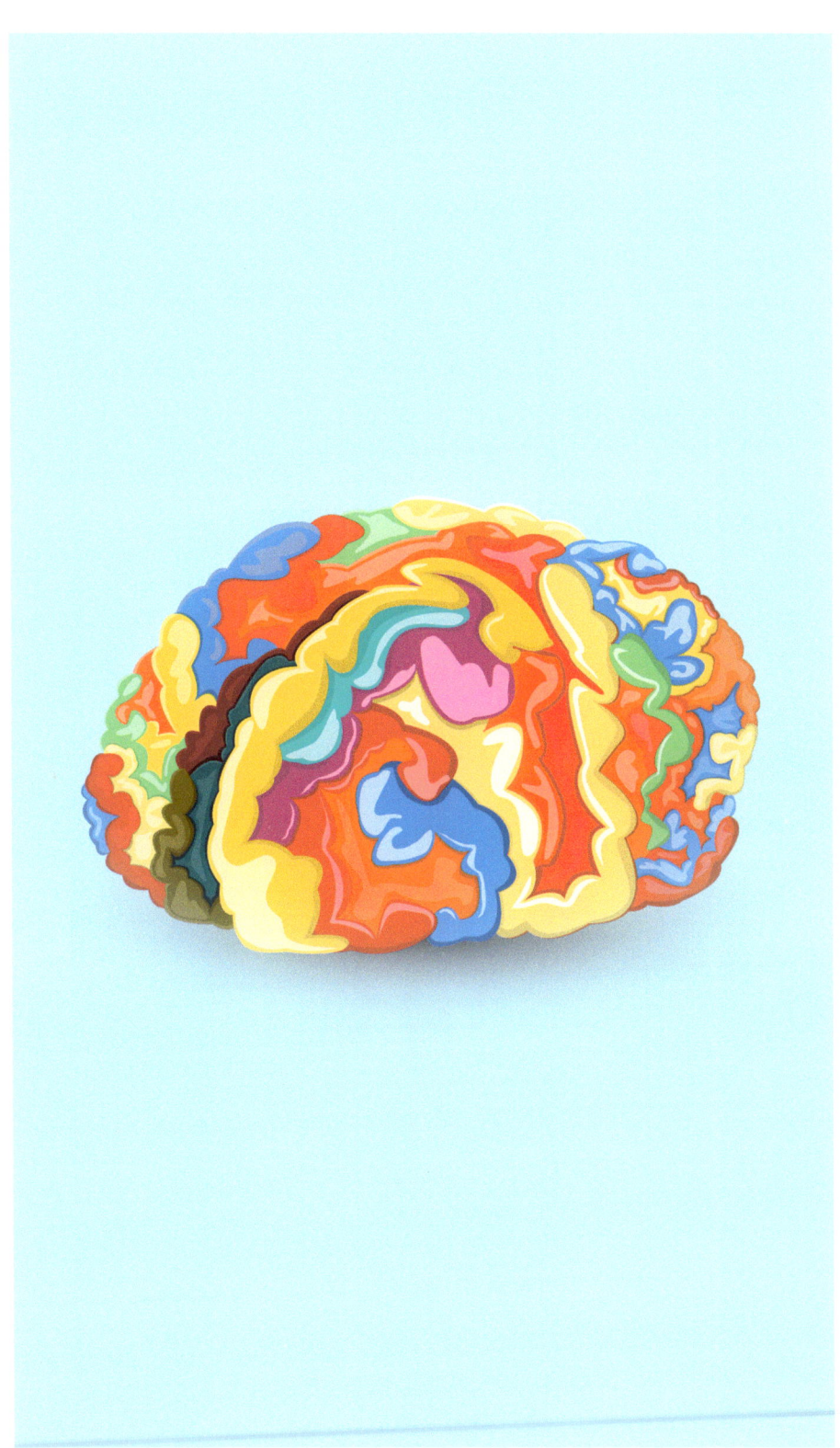

Brand yourself

Think of yourself as a brand – that way, you are selling the brand and not yourself.

Create an image that presents you in the way you wish people to perceive you.

That way, you can package your work consistently.

Design the image yourself.

Designing it yourself means being able to update it easily and it means that you are able to design for the most demanding client: yourself.

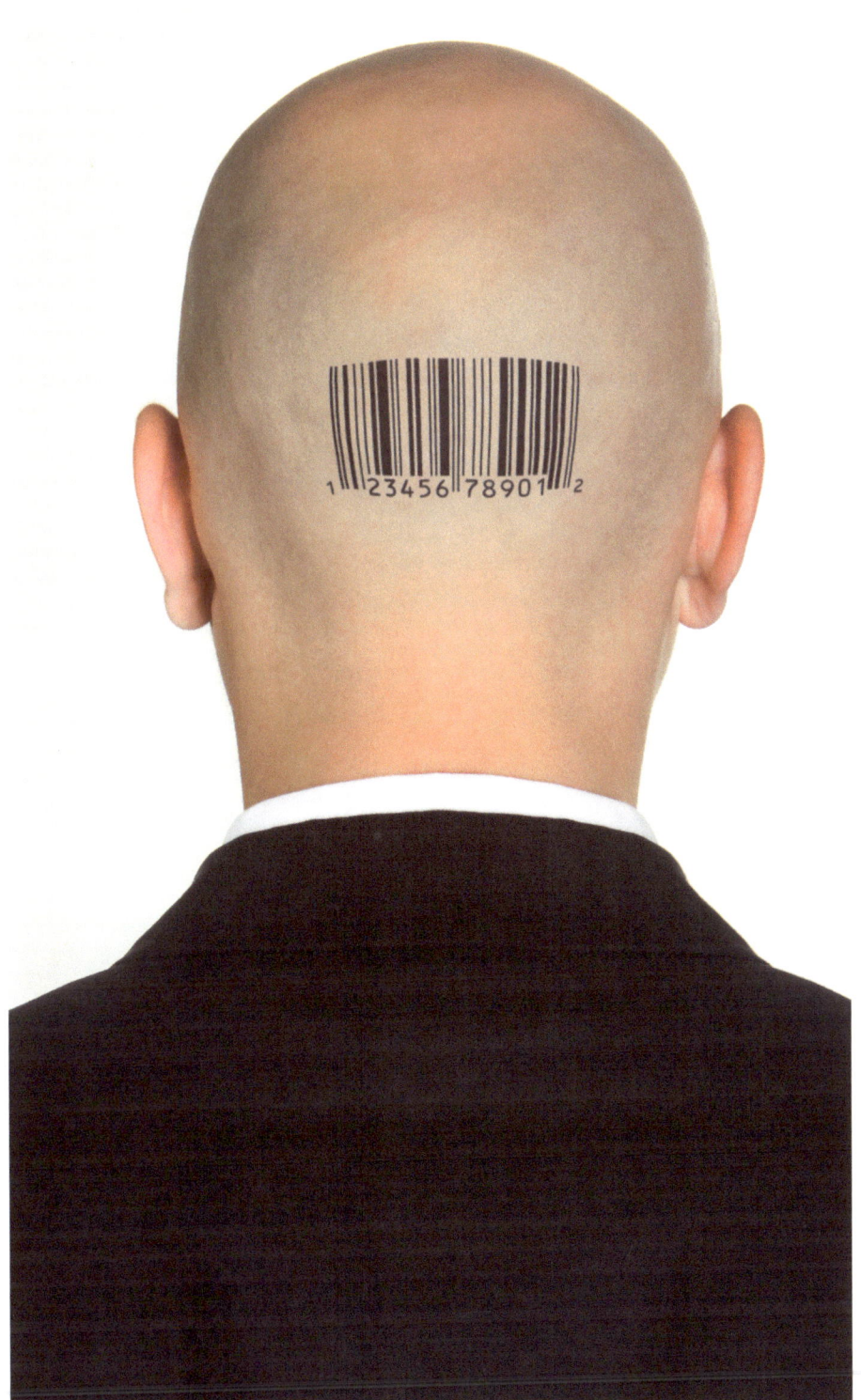

Label yourself

You may already know that talent is not enough, but did you know that sometimes it's too much.
The multitalented are still not accepted.
You have to fit into a box, and the box has to have a label.
The rule is one label per person, so choose the label carefully – it comes with a prize. You may have to carry it and its prize for a while.

Get a business card

Design a business card and make it memorable:
• add an image
• add your name
• add the role you are pursuing – junior editor, junior compositor, audio assistant, etc.
• add your mobile number
• add your email address
• add your website
Make a thousand copies and give them to everyone you meet.

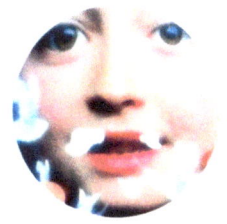

KLAUDIJA CERMAK
VISUAL EFFECTS ARTIST

+44 (0) 123 456 789
www.klaudijacermak.com
klaudija@klaudijacermak.com

Create a one page CV

However you lay out your CV, keep it clear and to the point:
• your name
• your contact details
• your job title
• your skills
• your education
• your work experience
• your credits
• your awards
• your interests (list at least one that involves teamwork)

P.S. Add a personal statement at the top of the CV. Keep it short – three to four lines that describe in a positive way your key skills, experience, personal qualities and your career objectives. If you can tweet, you can do this!

Write a cover letter

The cover letter should be one A4 page long. It is effectively a selling exercise. You are selling yourself!

1. It needs to be addressed to the right person. Find out who it is! It may be someone in HR department or a facility manager or…

2. It needs to be concise and to the point.

3. Start by stating the vacancy you are applying for.

4. List your relevant qualities, skills and experience that make you suitable for the job.

5. Describe your aspirations and what you can contribute to the company.

6. Demonstrate some knowledge of the company.

7. Show that you are passionate about your work.

8. End by asking for the opportunity to show your work in person.

Your spelling and grammar need to be immaculate or the letter will end up straight in the bin. Remember – attention to detail!

Edit a one minute showreel

One minute? Well, that is the maximum attention span of the people viewing it.
Remember, they receive dozens of showreels a day.
They are busy – and very tired, too.
If you need to show longer pieces of work or shot breakdowns, place them after
the short dynamic edit of your best work.
Put only your best work on, even if it is just one piece of work.
Anything else will dilute the showreel.
This is the one time in life you are allowed to be ruthless.

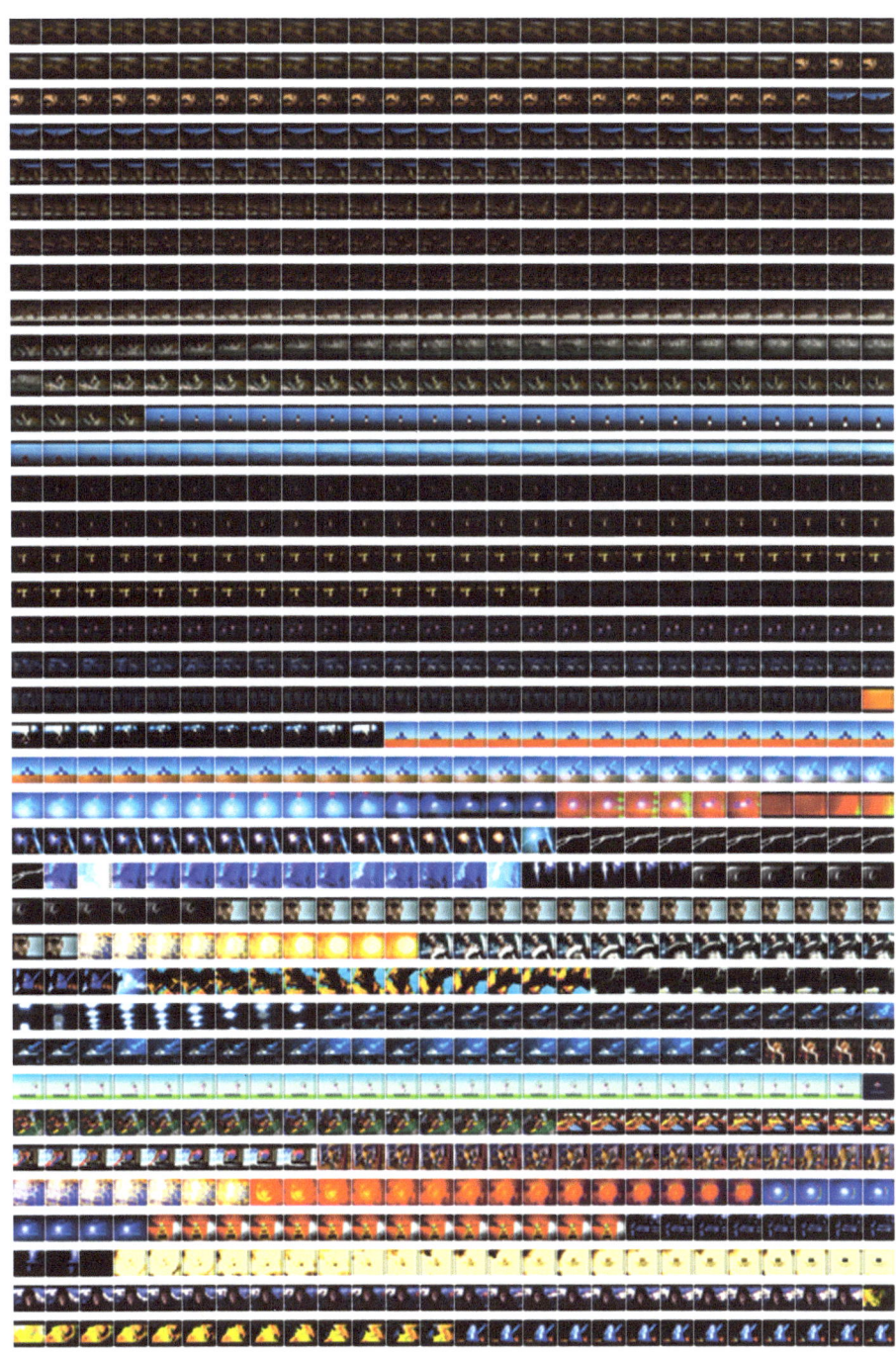

Build a nice simple website

The advantage of a website is that it is there for everyone to see anytime, anywhere. It saves time and money.

It frees you from making endless copies of the showreel and your CV.

And, most importantly, it saves you from queuing at post office counters, however much fun that may sometimes be – or however much fun the post office would like us believe it is.

With so many ready-made templates on the Web, a website is easy to set up and easy to update.

The joy is that, after you have set it up, you can add it to the social networking sites, and join the global network of hungry people like you.

Double esspresso to go

This is exactly what you need before the interview because however well prepared you are, you need to be sharp too.

An unexpected question may pop up – it always does.

When I went for an interview to a facility in Soho, after having a baby, I was asked by the chairman of the company:

'What would you do if your child had an accident? Would you just rush off and leave the clients behind?'

I thought for a minute, desperately searching for the right answer, the one that would preserve my dignity.

'No, I would take them with me', I said.

So remember, the interview is for your benefit too.

However much you want the job, you have to assess if this is the company that you really wish to work for.

Being an employee

This is usually a first step to building your career.

Joining a company means relative financial stability.

Financial stability means that you can concentrate on your job, which gives you the opportunity to develop and broaden your skills. After all you are, hopefully, surrounded by people more knowledgeable than yourself.

1. You get to learn how to work well in the team.
2. You get a chance to build a client base and a reputation for yourself.
3. You get a chance to make yourself indispensable.
4. Most importantly, you have none of the headaches of being freelance.

Being freelance

There is nothing free about being freelance, because you are either working or looking for work.

Gone are the days when you could survive by working a few days a month and spending the rest of the time browsing through bookshops or just chatting to strangers in cafés.

Being freelance means being part of a largely unprotected workforce in an unregulated labour market.

The volatility of the film tax breaks, the slashed budgets and the ever-increasing demand for higher profits have all contributed to freelancers' worsening work conditions.

The only time it's worth being freelance is if you need the free time to do something else, or if you don't need the money and are doing it for fun.

Setting a freelance rate

You can't get a permanent job, you have nothing else to do and you do need the money. Then it's time to set your rate.

$A/B = C$

$C/D = E$

A = gross annual salary of a full time person

B = the number of months you are likely to work

C = your monthly salary

D = 20 working days

E = your daily rate

If a person in full-time, permanent employment, doing the equivalent job, is paid £36,000 per year – which is roughly £3,000 per month – your daily rate should be at least £200, because on average as a freelancer you are unlikely to work more than nine months a year. You also don't reap any other benefits of the full-time person such as a pension, private health insurance, life insurance, a mobile phone or any other perks they may enjoy. Plus your outgoings are greater, as you have to pay for client entertaining, your promotion and any additional training and equipment you may require, though some of these are tax deductible. You should also check how much your fellow freelancers are charging. You wouldn't want to undercut them, for the simple reason that you wouldn't want them to undercut you.

Freelance contracts

If you are offered a freelance contract, it means that the company is likely to give you work for longer than five days and perhaps for up to a year. In this case, you will most likely not be paid the gross amount but will be taxed at source under PAYE. This is very inconvenient, because you are effectively paying tax in advance and you often have insufficient spare money to fall back on after the contract expires, while you are looking for another contract. It may be time to start lobbying your MP about this. In the meantime, talk to an accountant. Other things to look out for in the contract are:

• the duration of the contract
• the rate of pay
• the holiday entitlement
• the maximum working hours
• the sickness benefit
• the overtime pay
• the pay date
• the credit (ensure you are getting a credit if working on film or TV programme)
• the notice period

For example, a notice period of one week is quite unacceptable on long-term contracts, as it leaves you with too little time to secure the next project and to have continuity in earnings. Always try to negotiate.

Organising a freelance life

- register with recruitment agencies
- join professional groups and associations
- keep promoting yourself
- keep in touch with everyone
- do occasional favours for free
- get public liability insurance
- get a good accountant who understands the industry
- keep all receipts
- invoice promptly
- put at least 25% of your earnings aside if paid gross, which hopefully you won't need to touch until you get a tax bill
- buy any tools of the trade that you can charge for
- use your free time wisely

P.S. Cold-call the companies you wish to work for. Keep emailing the link to your CV and to your showreel and – call again.

The ultimate goal

"When a man tells you that he got rich through hard work, ask him: 'Whose?'"
*Don Marquis**

If you haven't read Marx, then any decent accountant will tell you that you can't make money unless you own the means of production, which in your case is a computer and the software – and employed people.
If you are not driven by money, or you think that exploiting other people's work for profit is wrong, even better, you can set up a social enterprise company.
Because, it's not just about the money.
It's about the ability to control one's destiny and the ability to shape one's future.

*http://quotationsbook.com/quote/42372 [Accessed 10.02.2012.]

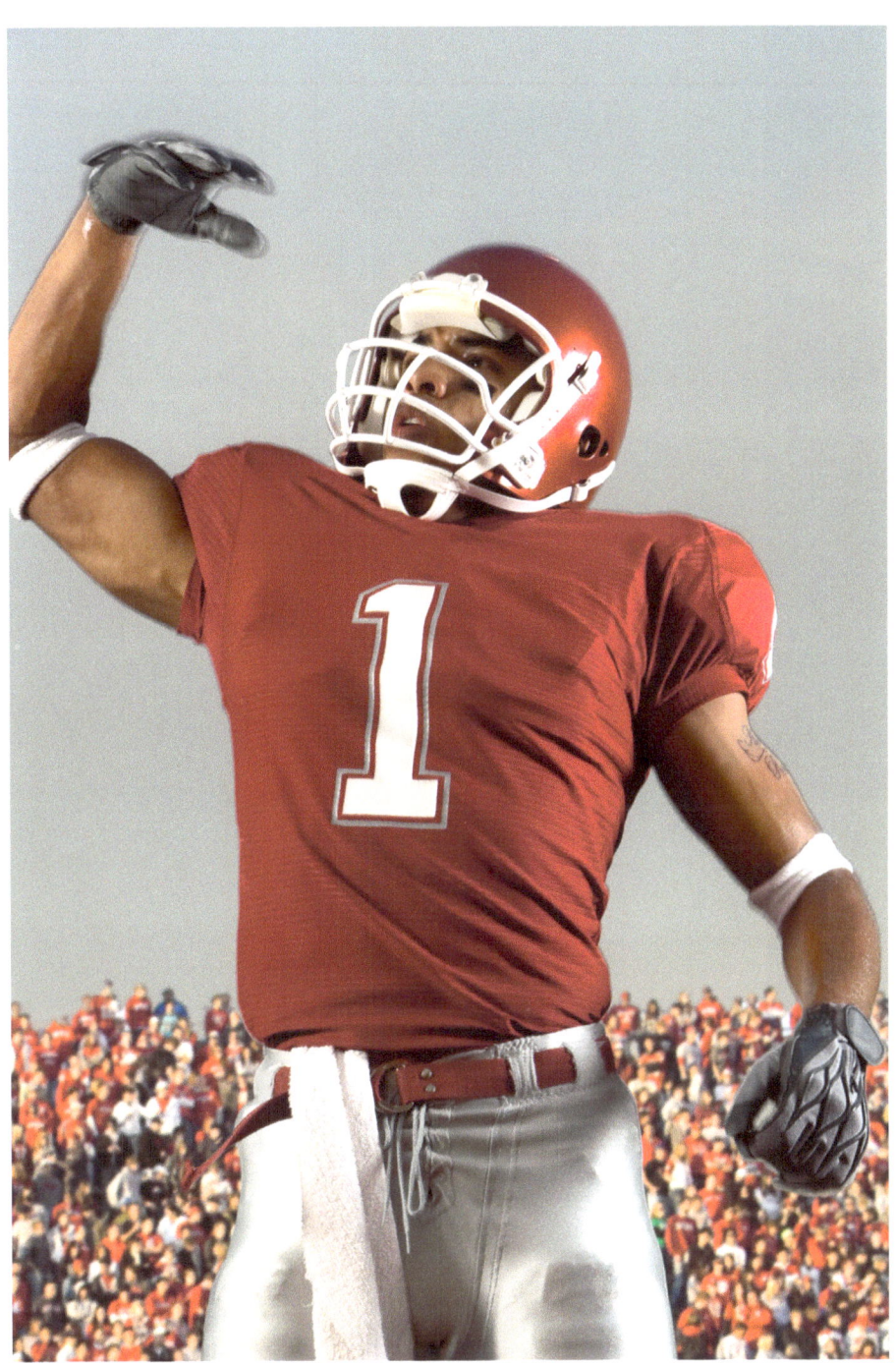

© Hemera/Hemera/Thinkstock

RULES FOR SURVIVAL

Rules are made to be broken

At the beginning of my career, a colleague told me:
'You can't combine these two colours. They don't go.'
At first, I was taken aback.
Immediately after, I felt exhilarated.
I didn't know the rules.
I was free!
Ten years later, these two colours were the 'in' grade.
The TV screens were flooded with brown/turquoise commercials.
Twenty years later I enrolled at St Martin's.
I wanted to learn all the rules.

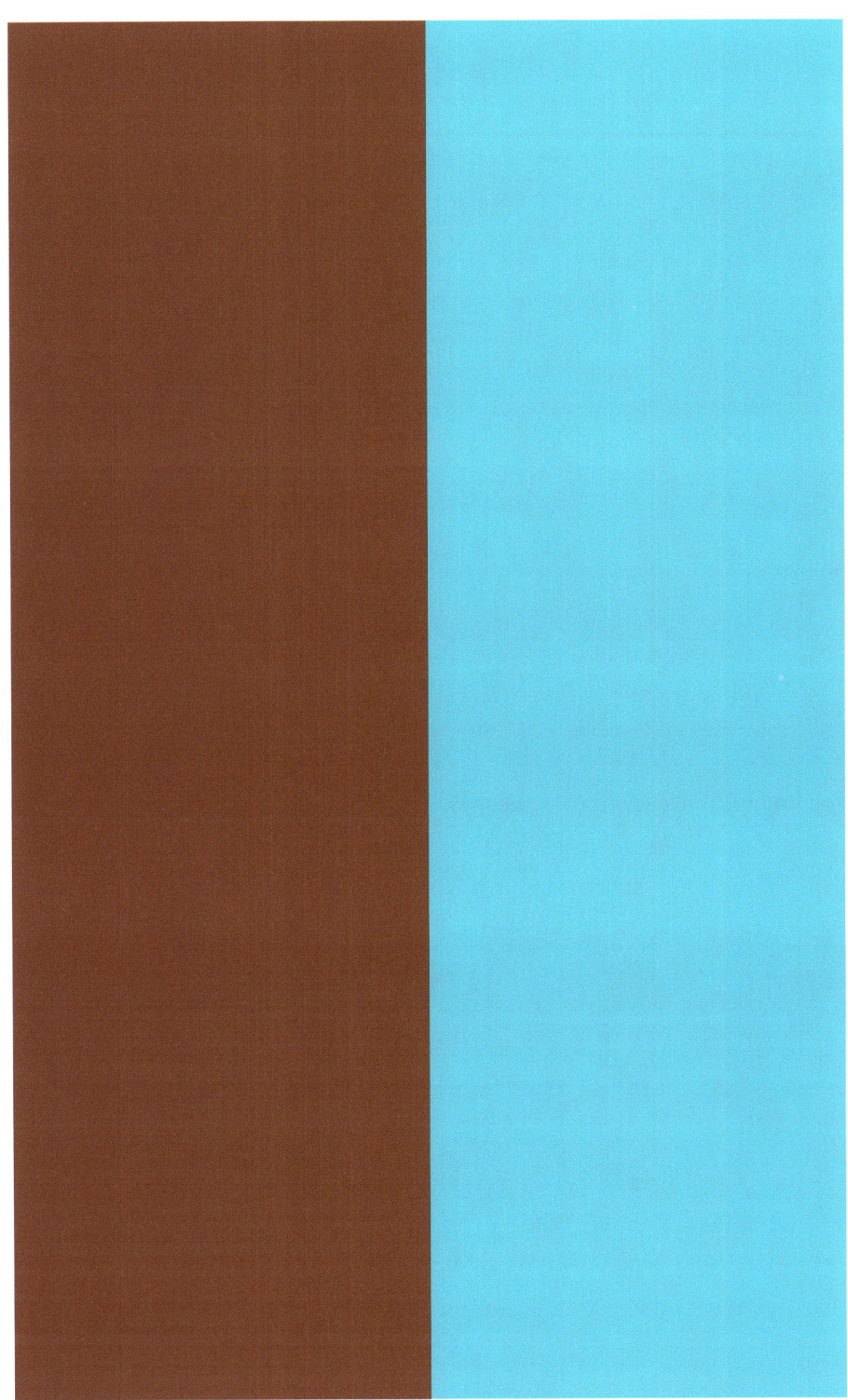

Client is God

There is one good reason for this – he is holding the purse strings.

However, in advertising post-production there may be up to 20 people in the room with you and, in effect, they are all gods. And, even though you are all working on the same commercial, everyone has a different opinion because everyone has a different agenda.

• The creatives want to win an award so they can get a bonus.

• The account manager wants to keep the client happy without upsetting the creatives.

• The TV producer wants to keep the creatives happy without upsetting the client.

• The director wants to make a break into Hollywood.

• The producer is desperate to keep within the budget.

• The editor wants to be a commercials director.

• The client wants to increase the sales.

And you?

You just want to keep everyone happy.

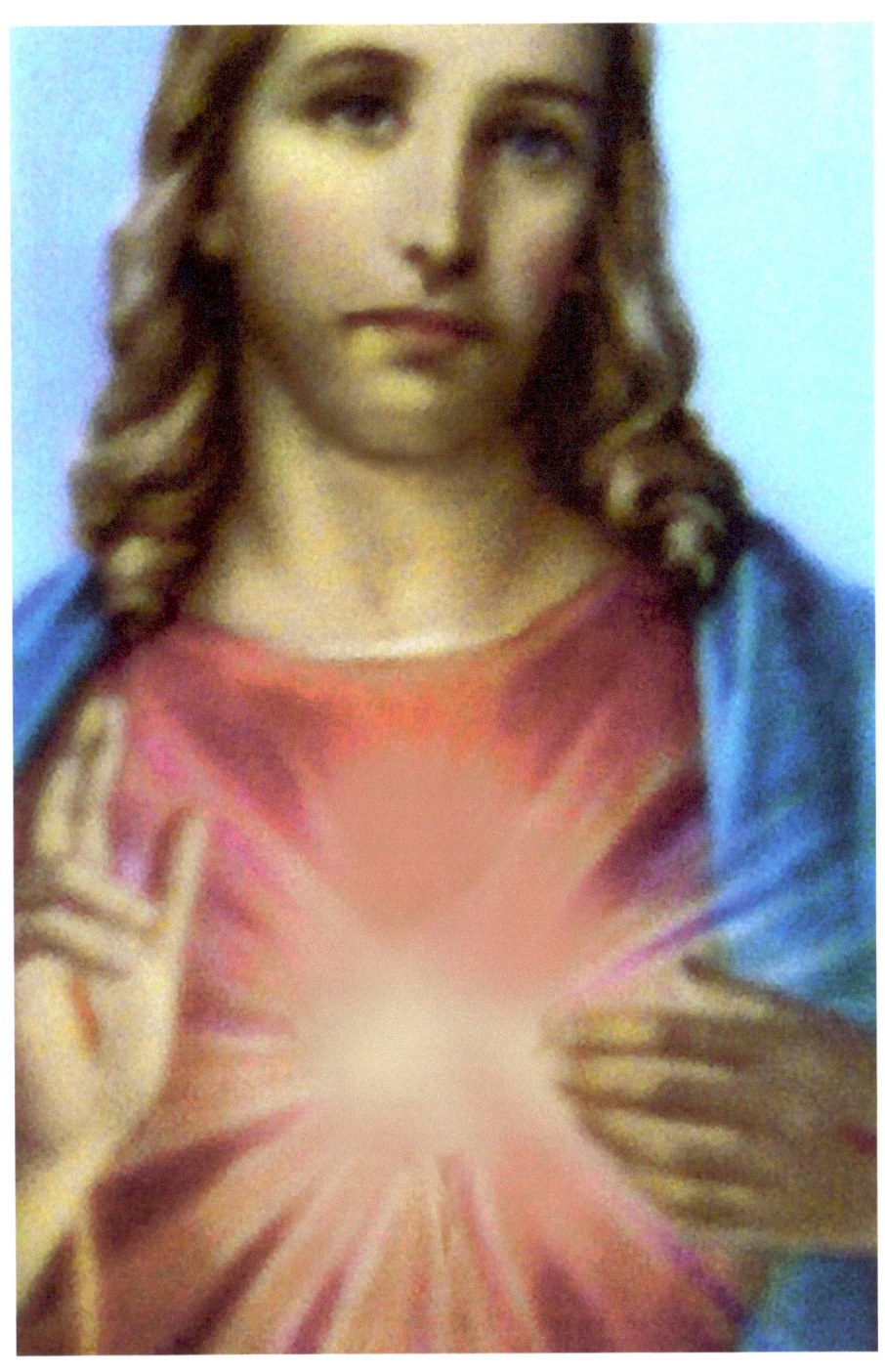

Manners will get you everywhere

In post-production, one is often surrounded by a bunch of clients. Each of them wants to make a contribution, so everyone has a comment or a suggestion.

You have to take each suggestion into account, whoever offers it, however long it may take, or however confident you are that it's not going to work because you have tried it before.

The thing is, clients have to see it before they reject it or, sometimes, accept it. And if they ask for a slight, miniscule, change in colour and you then press a few buttons to get into the right menu to make the change, and before actually making it, you hear a voice saying 'That's much better', under no circumstances should you say, 'But I haven't done anything yet.'

What good would that do?

Be polite and just get on with it.

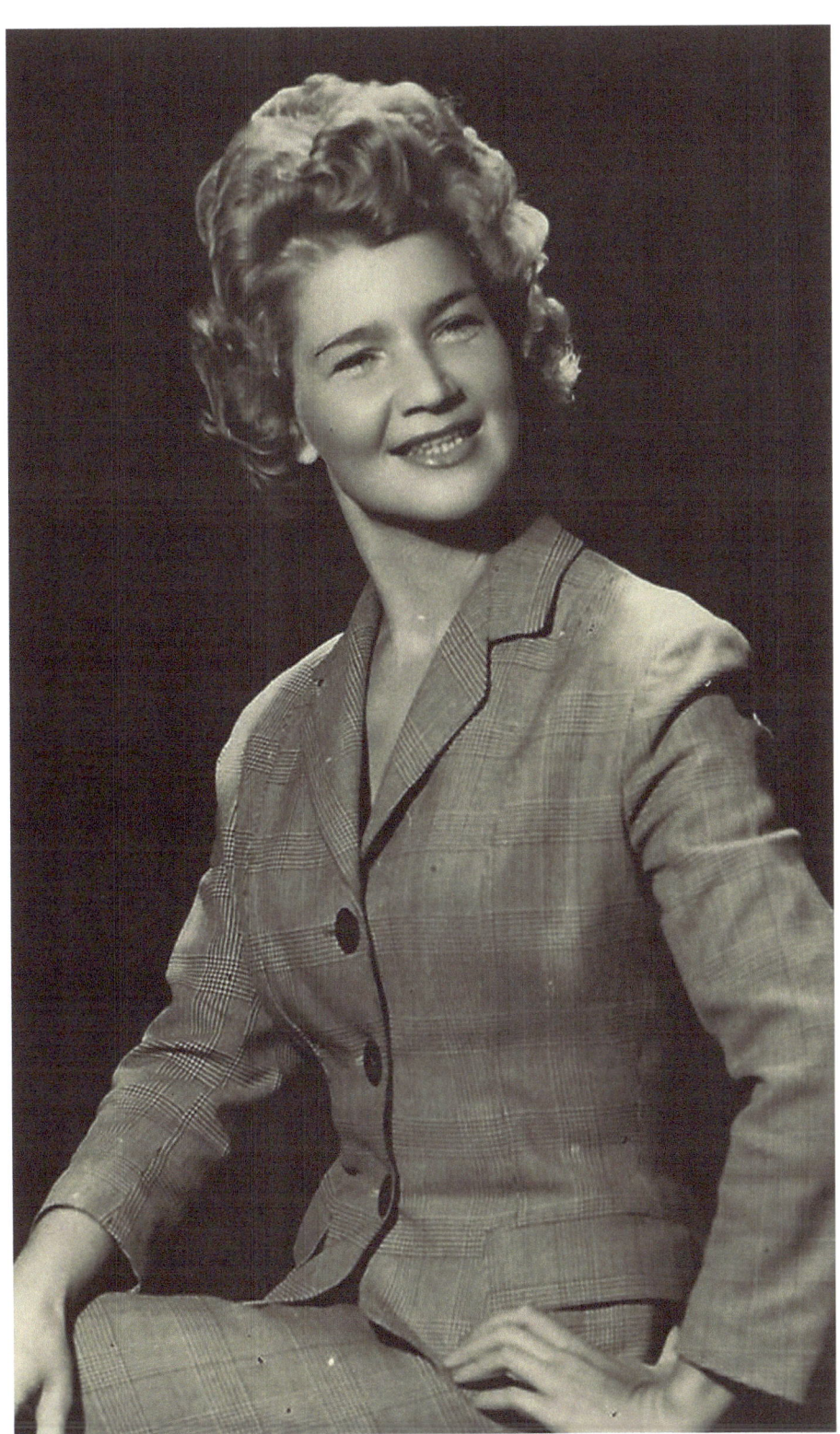

Black sheep white sheep

Joining a company brings another dilemma.
Should you blend in or should you stand out?
And if so, how much?
Just a little bit – a tiny, little bit.
You need to get noticed but you don't want to cause envy.
And, by the way, conformity is 'in', eccentricity is 'out'.

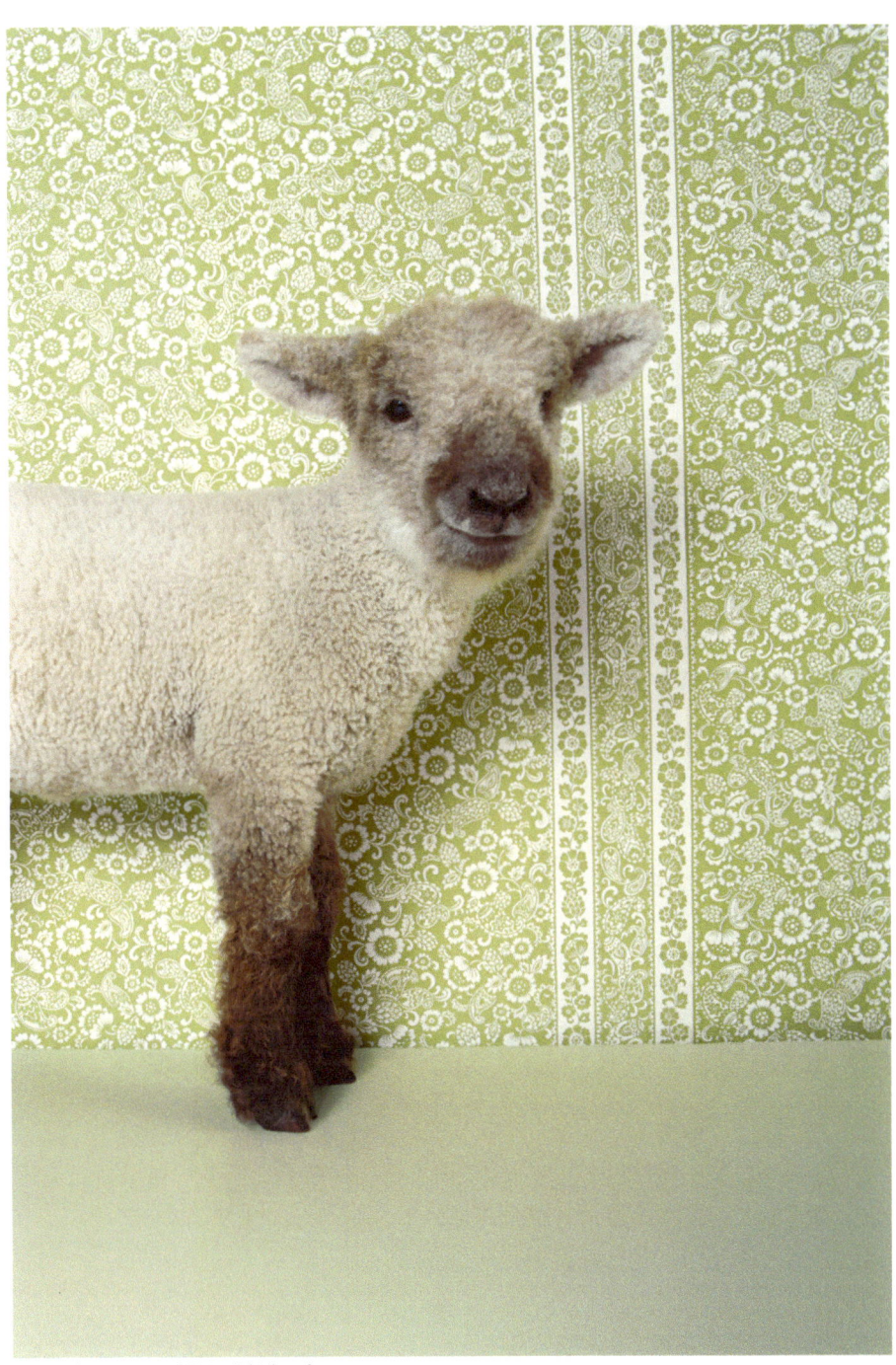

© Digital Vision/Digital Vision/Thinkstock

It's who you know...

Networking is still the biggest contribution you can make to your career.
All the best jobs are won by the word of mouth – most are never advertised.
You are more likely to hear about a job from someone you know in a pub than by seeing an ad.
You are also more likely to get an interview if your friend from the pub has recommended you.
With the industry's long hours and people's constant migrations from company to company, it used to be a challenge keeping up with former colleagues - not anymore.
Add them as friends on Facebook.
Connect with them on Linkedin.
Follow them on Twitter.
And meet them in the real world.

And how well you get on with people

Getting on well with people means that you are able to be part of a team.
Good team players get jobs, not necessarily because they are brilliant at what they do, it's more often because they are 'a great laugh' or 'fun to be with' while also good at what they do.

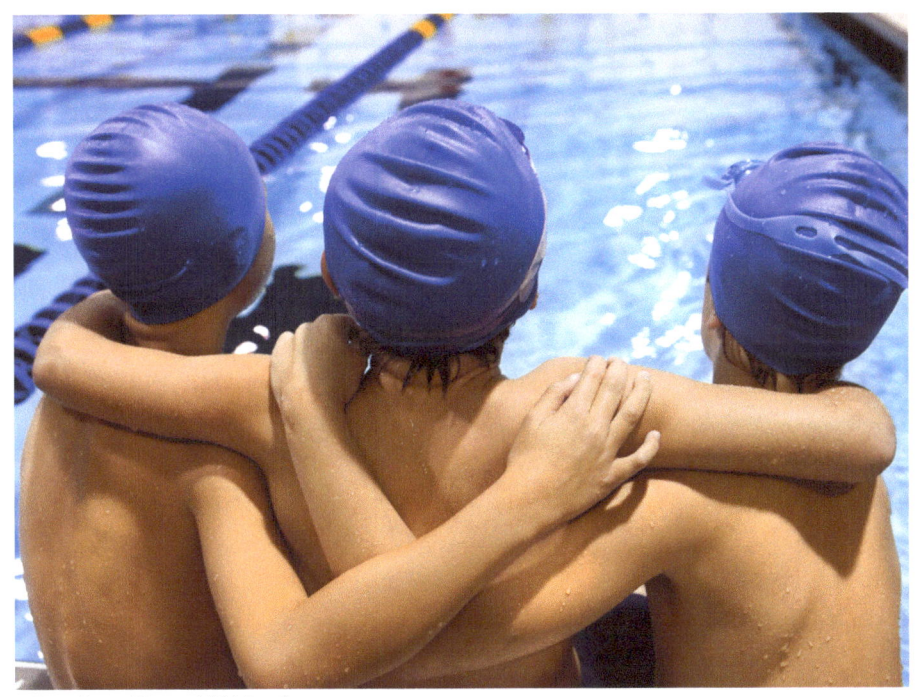

© Jupiterimages/Comstock/Thinkstock

If you don't ask you will never know

There is nothing wrong about not knowing.
What's wrong is not trying to learn.
The industry is full of people who have bluffed their way through.
You don't want to be one of them.
Ask questions, keep learning and keep the industry moving: onwards and upwards. Don't forget, knowledge is power!

Throw yourself into the deep end

Even when you think you may drown.
That's the best way to learn and it's the quickest way to find out if you are up to the job.
I was once asked to take over a job, which had gone wrong.
It was at the beginning of my career, I wasn't very experienced and I was probably not much better than the previous artist, but I got on well with the clients.
I made them laugh with my East European jokes and I sailed through the job.
The next day, I got a bunch of flowers from the clients and a job offer from the company.
If you don't jump, you may never know.

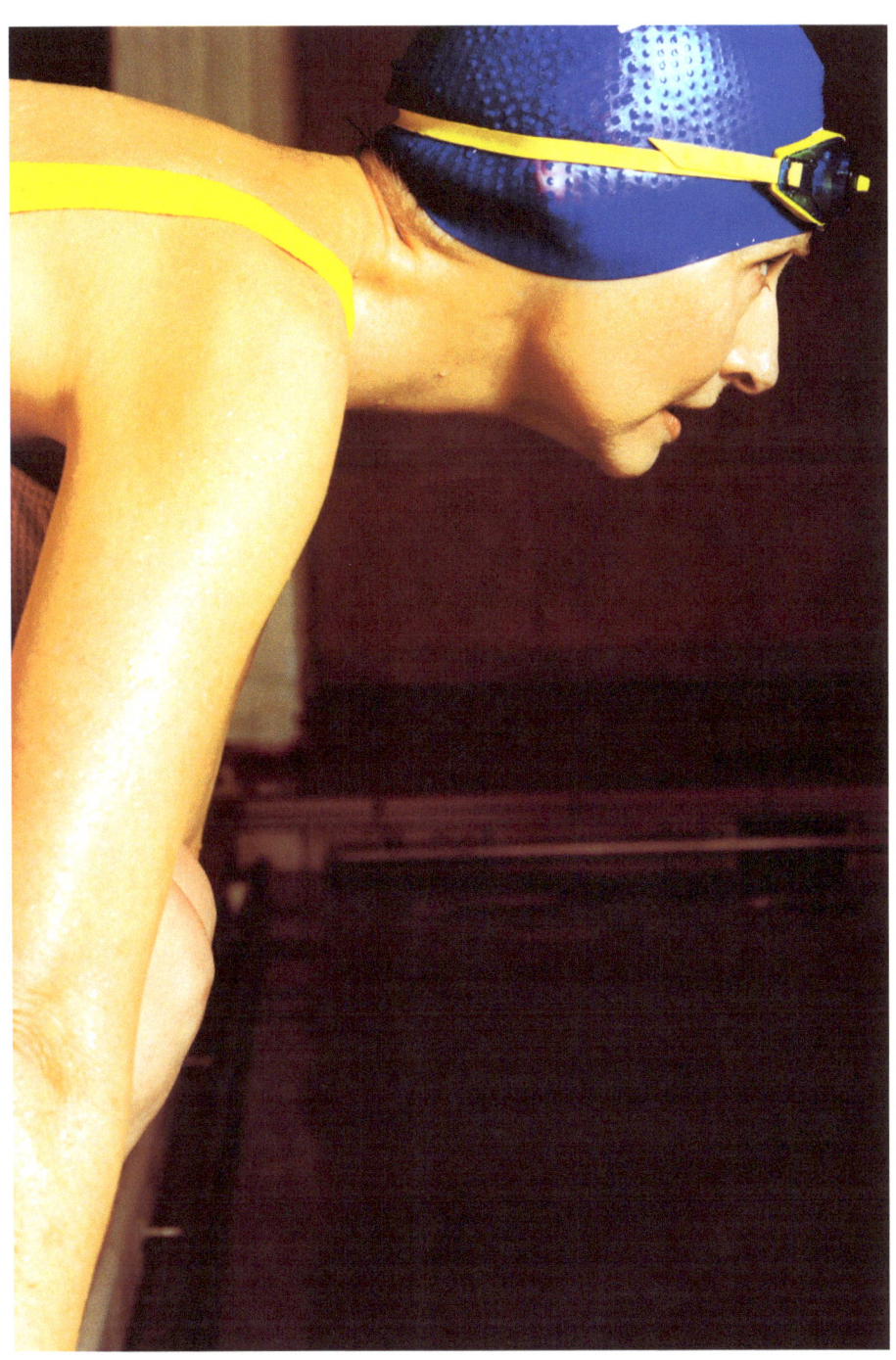

Keep up

You have mastered the software.

You have the job you wanted and you can do it with closed eyes.

Then a new software comes out.

Should you learn it?

You most definitely should.

Why?

Because the students are learning it and you don't want them to take your job, do you?

P.S. When I went for an interview in Soho, the MD asked me why I keep changing companies so often. I wasn't changing companies, I was moving to new hardware/software: from Supernova, Matisse, Rodin, Paintbox, Harry, Harriet, Henry, Flame, Combustion, Shake, FCP, Motion, Color, Nuke... and still going.

Always have a plan B

You got the job.

The clients love you.

Your colleagues love you.

The management loves you.

You can relax.

No, sorry, you can't. This is a perfect time to make a plan B because something is bound to go wrong with plan A.

So plan your escape route now. Because one day, when you want to escape or they want to let you go, you need to know where and how.

P.S. Never put all your eggs into one basket.

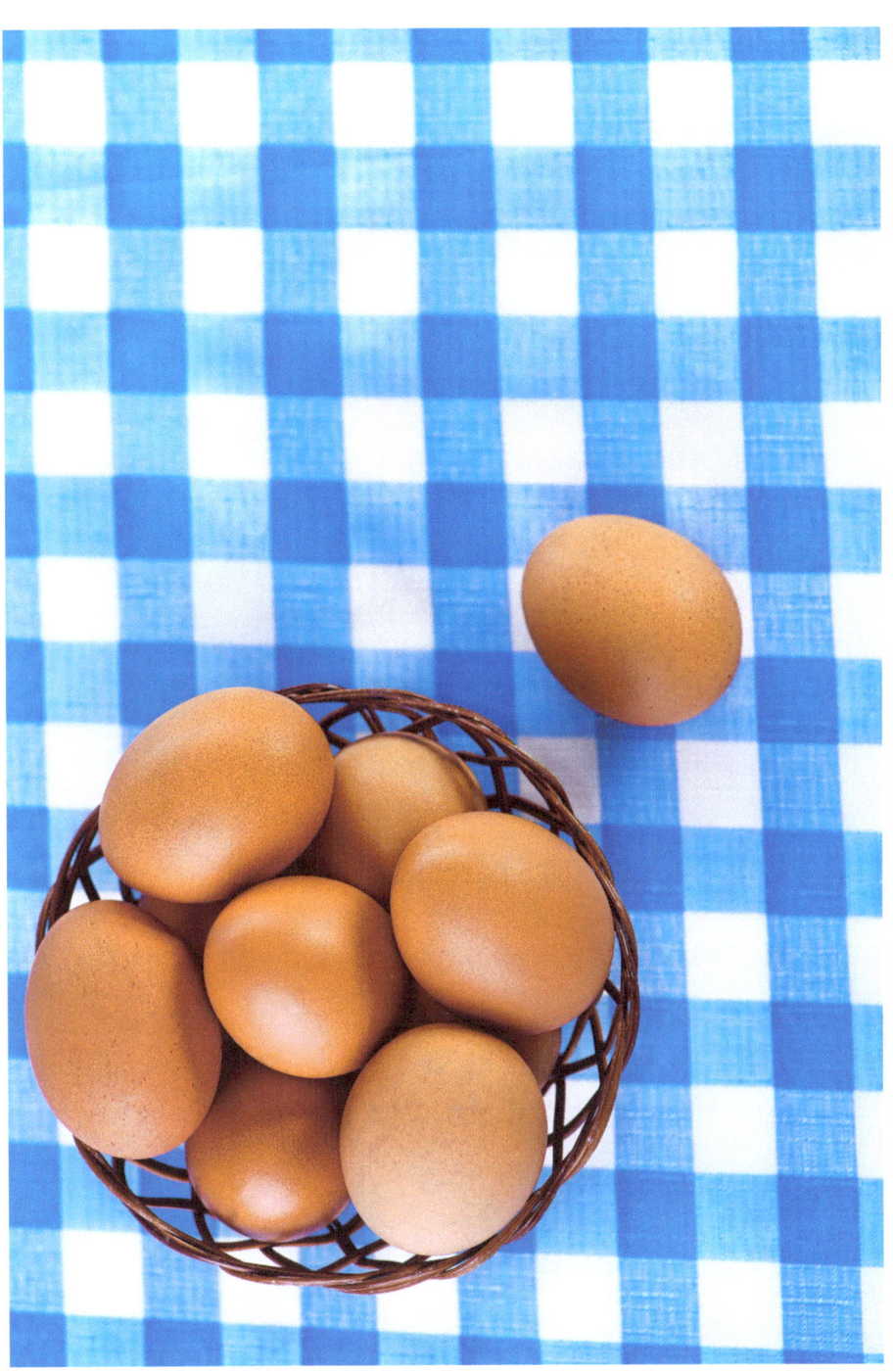

To pitch or not to pitch?

After spending months creating your showreel, you are asked to pitch an idea for a title sequence or a promo.

They have seen your showreel - can't they see you can do the job?

Apparently not.

Unfortunately, gone are the days when you could present an idea scribbled on a napkin from Groucho's.

Nowadays, pitching requires a lot of time and a lot of resources.

Some pitches require a moving image, too. So one has to make it, to win the right to make it.

It's crazy, but true.

My advice is, don't pitch unless you're getting paid for it.

If you are not getting paid, the client is not serious enough and most often, he will walk off with your idea and make it with someone else.

P.S. Or simply pitch on a napkin from Groucho's.

Ideas that don't get through

Some ideas don't get through because they are bad.

But not all great ideas get through either.

Some of the best ones are never realised.

Sometimes they are just too original.

Most clients have no wish to create something new and original.

They are looking for something that has been tried and tested – something new that has already been done: something 'in' – an existing idea modified.

The thing is, if it's 'in', it's already 'out'.

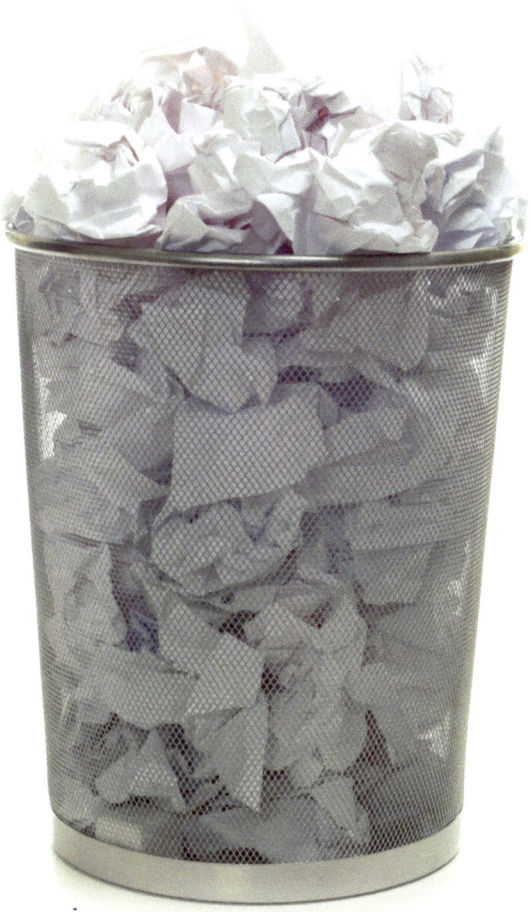

© Hemera/Hemera/Thinkstock

Reject one – 'que sera sera'

Beautiful lyrical shots of children playing.

Boy is pushing a wheel with a stick.

Subtitle: Birmingham 1980.

Girl is swinging on a swing.

Subtitle: Liverpool 1966.

Boy is playing with strings of wool on his fingers.

Subtitle: Walthamstow 1950.

Girl is carrying a doll's house across a field.

Subtitle: Exeter 1923.

Boy is blowing soap bubbles.

Subtitle: Luton 1966.

Little girl is placing a crown of daisies on her head, using the camera as a mirror.

Subtitle: Stratford 1931.

As camera pulls out, girl's face seamlessly morphs into old woman's face and reveals a group of homeless people.

Subtitle:: London 2012.

Title: You, too, could join the growing community of homeless people.

Reject two – 'imagine'

'Imagine being able to restore the eyesight of 10,000 people in India.
Subtitle: £100,000
Imagine driving to Bosnia and delivering artificial limbs to 7,000 amputees.
Subtitle: £400,000
Imagine trekking through Africa and buying camels for 1,000 poor families.
Subtitle: £300,000
Imagine taking a train to St Petersburg with warm clothes for 30,000 street children.
Subtitle: £300,000
Imagine riding through Mongolian tundra and building homes for 100 nomad families.
Subtitle: £500,000
Imagine doing all that and still having money to spare.
Imagine being able to change the world.
Don't just dream. Play.
Lottery logo.

I entered these two ideas for different competitions.
They were both short-listed, but neither was chosen to be made into an ad.
The first one was for a social awareness competition, though to be fair another of my ideas was chosen instead.
The second one was in reply to a client's brief to make playing the lottery attractive to 16-24 year-olds.
P.S. I am in no way suggesting that these ideas are great, or even good. I am just reminding you that not all ideas get realised.

Presenting the idea

The best way to present an idea is with a script, a drawn storyboard and a mood board.

A mood board is a selection of images that suggest the possible ways the film could look.

Why offer more than one look?

Because, clients need to be given a choice.

They need to think that they are in control.

If you are smart, you can lead them to choose your favourite one.

If you are not, well then.

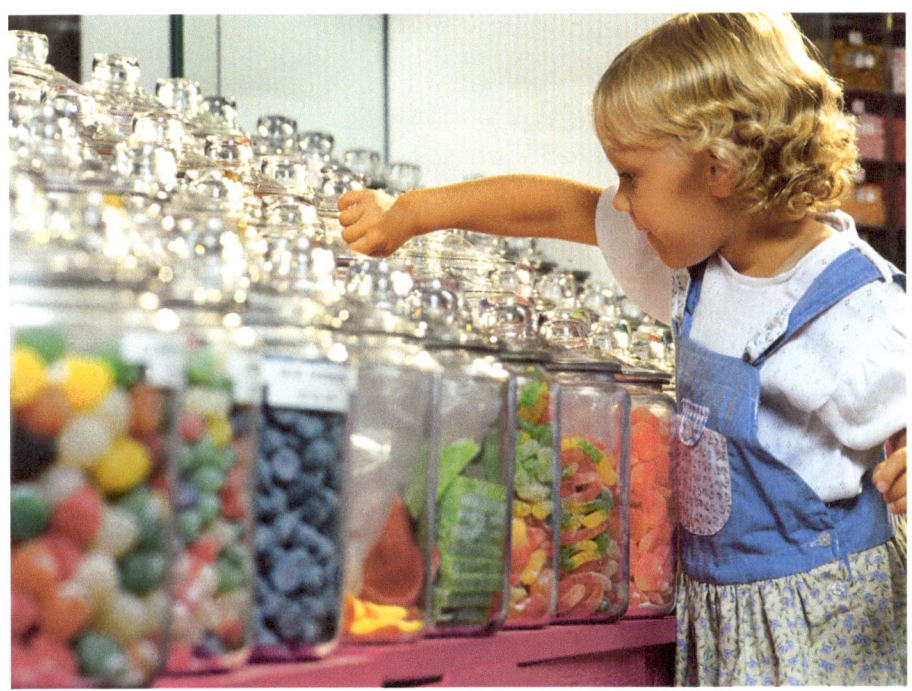

© Comstock/Comstock/Thinkstock

Pay and feed the crew

Your idea got through - now you get to make it.

The problem is, as usual, the idea is greater than the budget, so you are thinking of not paying the shoot crew.

Reconsider!

A good reason for paying the crew - besides the ethical one - is that they can concentrate on the project without worrying where the money for the next bill is coming from.

Another good reason is that you get to choose the people you work with.

Assembling the right team for a project increases its chance of a success - as does keeping the crew happy.

And there is nothing that will keep them happier than a nice juicy shepherds pie, followed by apple crumble with custard.

This is because, often, the most memorable thing about the shoot is the food.

Small budget – big ideas

People are always tempted to make a bigger film than the budget allows.

The client walks in, clutching a Star Wars DVD.

The DVD is parked on the shot that took months to make and cost hundreds of thousands of dollars.

He wants to replicate it, only he has very little money and a week to do it in.

He promises to bring the next job with a decent budget.

Should you do it?

Almost certainly not.

There is no way you will be able to get the shot to a decent standard, so he will leave unhappy and his next job is going to the Far East, anyway.

Worry about the pack-shot

In advertising, most of the brands' clients would be more than happy to fill the thirty seconds' screen time with a pack-shot (end product shot in a commercial). So, when the footage lands on your computer, start working on the pack-shot first. It is often the only shot – beside the other product shots – that the client will carefully examine in the end.

When the client walks in at 6.00 p.m. on the last day, his main concern will be how his brand is looking. If you leave the pack-shot to last, you are bound to be still tidying it up at 4.00 a.m., as the director has spent the whole week perfecting the film for his showreel.

Making it look as good – or preferably better – than the one we pick up from the shop's shelves can take a long time.

And when that is done, it's time for the copy (text).

Positioning it a little to the left, a little to the right, a tad up or, a tad down can take another few hours.

And so, it is sunrise.

Keep smiling

As in any other segment of society, you will occasionally come across some unpleasant people.

The clients are no exception.

Some are bad mannered, some are incompetent, some are bullies, some can't make decisions and some are plainly rude.

Some clients will ignore you and some will shout at you - don't let it get to you.

Press a render button, get out and have a good cry in the loo, or take a walk around the block.

Have a cigarette.

But whatever you do, come back with a smile and keep going.

Because the next client is bound to be nice – I promise.

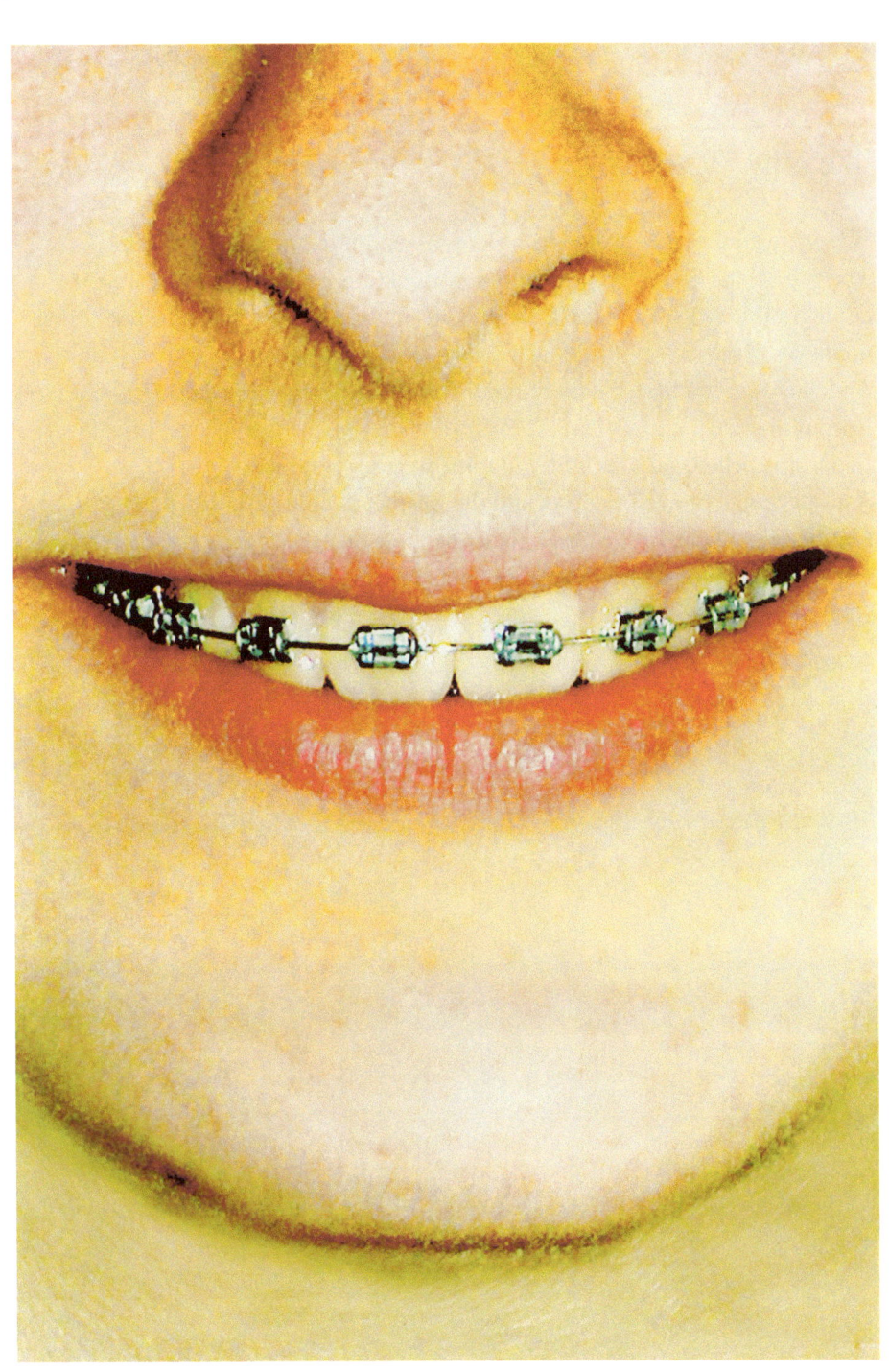

'It's only TV'

'We are just human – not robots quite yet – and humans make mistakes.

The good thing about working in post-production is that, when you erase the entire project at 1.00 a.m. by mistake, you can find comfort in the thought that nobody will die.

And, anyway, you have plenty of time – till the morning - to recreate it, so no harm done.

I once misspelled 'gales' as 'gails' on some weather graphics.

A lot of people phoned in upset and the weather people never hired me again.

On the bright side, I have never made the same mistake again.

P.S. Experience means that you have made your mistakes already.

Taking over a job gone wrong

You are asked to take over a job that's gone wrong.

What do you do?

You don't want to pick up a difficult job with a difficult client, and you don't want to undermine a colleague.

Most likely, however, the colleague will be relieved to be able to walk out of a difficult situation and will be more than happy to let someone else take over.

By being asked to take over, you are held in a higher esteem by the client, even though he doesn't know you and has never worked with you before.

The client will be more mellow and receptive to suggestions, so you will be able to complete the job more or less holding the strings.

In the end the client may hug you and your colleague will certainly buy you a drink.

The morning after

Open-day bookings don't seem as common now as in the 1980's and 1990's.

This is a 24-hour booking, but the client pays for ten hours only.

He is welcome to stay as long as it takes to finish the job – this can be till 9.00 a.m. the next morning.

It differs from 24/7, as it has no shift system.

The artist commencing the job is expected to complete it.

What's more, the artist may be expected to continue another session with a new client walking in at 9.00 a.m. the next day.

If it happens to you, sneak out before 9.00 a.m.

Switch off your phone, go for a good fry-up, then take a taxi home and get some sleep.

Beware of a knock on your door – it is another taxi driver, coming to take you back to work.

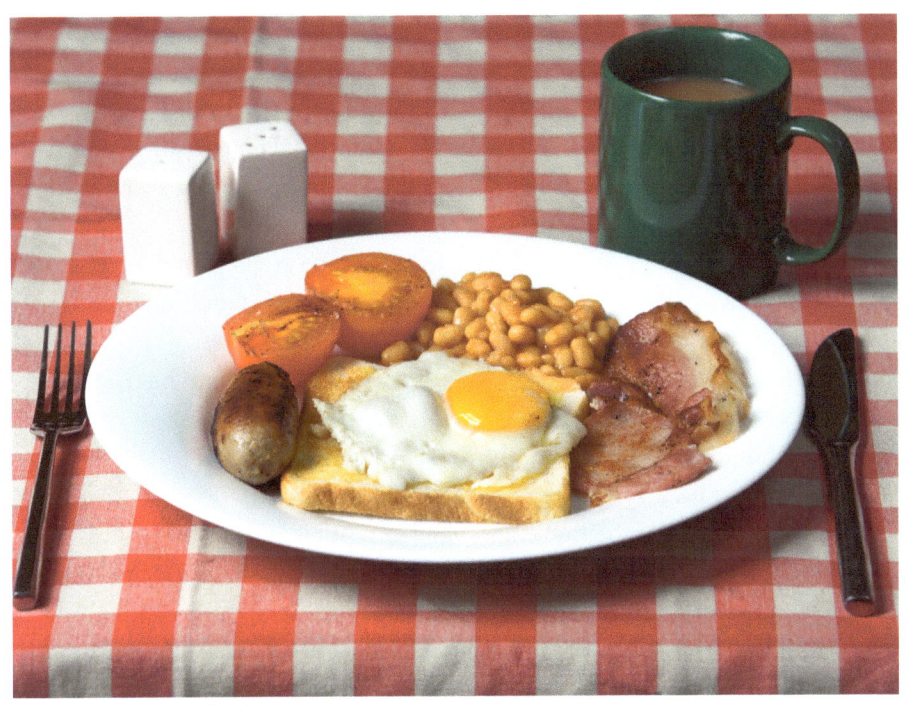

© iStockphoto/iStockphoto/Thinkstock

A taxi taking you home

After a long, hard day's work, all one wishes for is a nice, quiet ride home in a taxi. But taxi drivers are chatty and one is invariably drawn into a discussion about whether the Americans landed on the moon, the invasion of aliens or the rising crime rate.

I was expecting such a journey when I hailed a taxi one evening after work. A few minutes into the analysis of the safety of the Underground, a motorbike cut in front of us.

The taxi driver got annoyed and accelerated to catch up with him, but the biker moved into a separate lane in order to turn right.

My driver shouted an obscenity at him and sped off.

The biker turned back and started chasing us.

He caught up with us at the traffic lights and got off his bike.

My driver opened his window, spat at him, closed the window and locked his door – but not mine.

So the biker got in, through the passenger door, leaned over me and banged on the window separating the driver's part of the cabin from the passenger's one.

After a minute or so, he gave up, got out and left.

The taxi driver turned to me and said, 'There are some real nutters around.'

There certainly are.

So, pick your taxi driver with care.

Avoid the burnout

Forget the life – work balance – that's gone.

What you have to concentrate on is improving your workspace.

Working in front of the computer requires the following:

• a comfortable adjustable chair

• a desk of appropriate height

• a correctly positioned monitor

• the appropriate lighting

You must take regular ten-minute breaks every hour in order to stretch your body, refocus your eyes and wriggle your fingers.

P.S. And don't forget to get out and about at lunchtime.

Bullies bully

'Those who can, do. Those who can't, bully.'
www.bullyonline.org
In almost every workplace there is a bully;
the bullying is usually verbal or emotional.
Remember, bullies shouldn't be tolerated.
• They are counter-productive.
• They stop people getting on with their job.
• They reduce performance.
• They lose company money.
Money?
Now the management may do something about it.

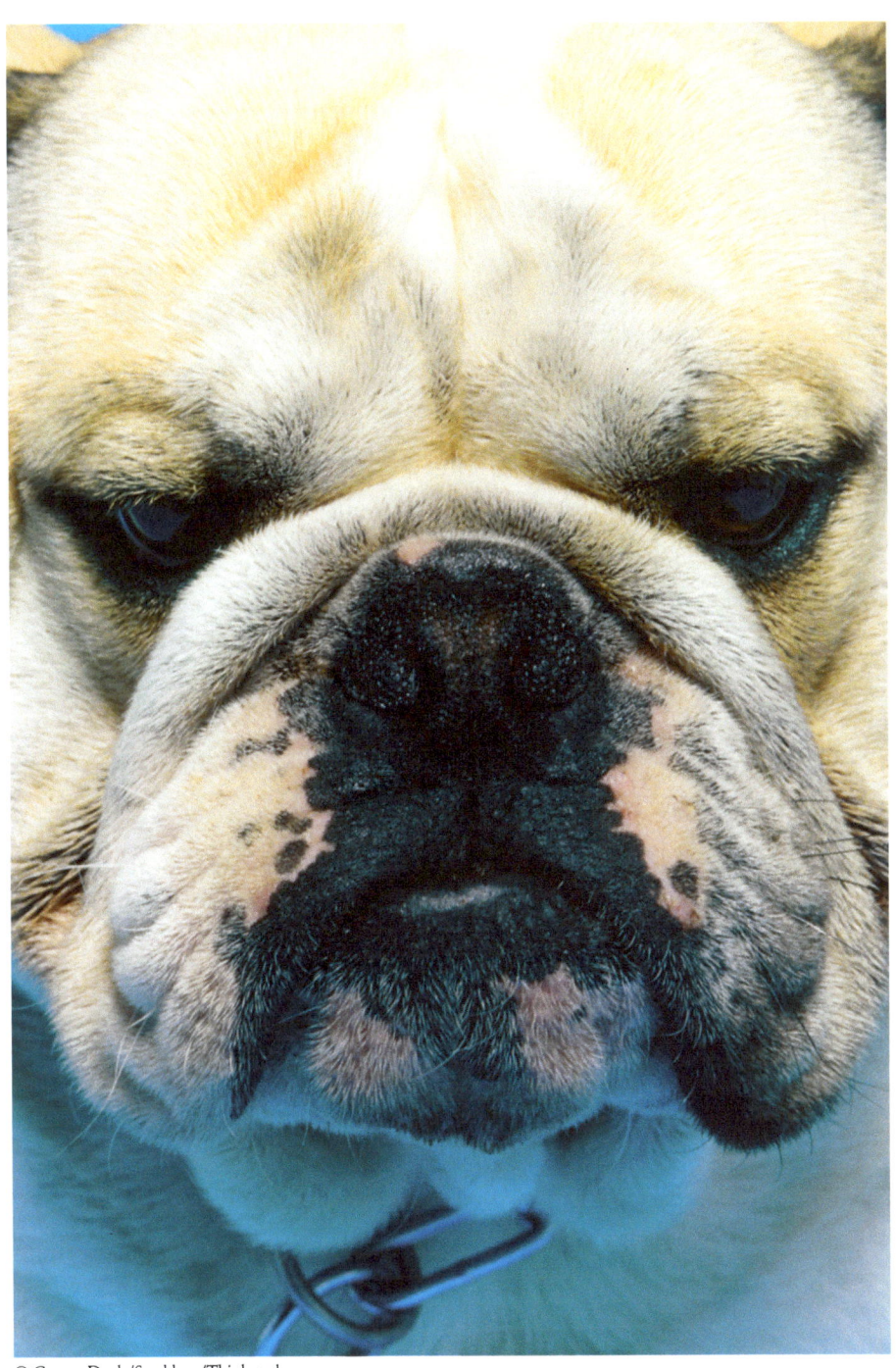

© George Doyle/Stockbyte/Thinkstock

Stop the programme credits!

Are they on fast-forward?

Is there no speed limit on them?

And now they are squeezed as well.

If you think that's bad, think again – no credit is much worse.

So, let's remind ourselves.

The programme credit is an acknowledgment of one's contribution to the programme.

Nothing more and nothing less.

Big deal!

But it is a big deal, because that is the main way of putting one's name around and getting the next job.

I worked on a television programme for six months, six to seven days a week.

I was quite surprised not to see my name at the end of the programme, but even more so when the caterer's name went by.

You see how important it is to feed the crew well!

Still, fight for the credit!

P.S. When working on big blockbuster films, you are not guaranteed a credit.

This is because the film studios have introduced some sort of credits quota for visual effects people (as there are too many). Of course, there are too many, as too many shots require too many effects in too short a time.

People should be given the credit or given the royalties.

For now, don't let go of the credit.

Awards

Awards are like one's age.

They don't seem important to you but they are important to others.

As with the lottery, in order to win, you have to play first.

So, the first step is to enter your work.

If other people are entering the work you have contributed to, make sure your name is included on the submission form. You would be amazed at how forgetful people can be.

Likewise, if you are entering the work yourself try not to 'forget' other people's contributions to it.

Freelancing abroad

At one stage or another, we all dream of working abroad and most often in a nice hot country.

Getting a freelance booking from abroad usually means that you are likely to be booked on a difficult job that the locals are either unable or unwilling to do.

The most important thing to remember is to make sure they book you into a four-star hotel at least.

When they work you to death – which they invariably will – at least there is decent room service to help you get going the next day.

I once took over a job from a freelancer who, after working for a day, returned to the hotel, emptied the mini bar and then took the first flight back to England the next day.

Of course, I didn't know this before I arrived but I could empathise with him after 20 clients walked in and argued throughout the session in a foreign language, banging their hands on the table.

Full-time abroad

Of course, when taking a full-time job abroad there are more things to consider: the contract, the language, the customs and the culture – and never under-estimate the value of the safety-net of your friends and family.

Even moving within the European Union is complicated enough.

You would think that most of the bureaucracy has been streamlined but, unbelievably, even the tax year dates are different within the countries of the EU.

Either the financial benefits or the quality of life have to be big enough to compensate for all the setbacks you are likely to encounter.

And if you don't know the language, believe me, it is no fun kneeling by the washing machine with a manual and a dictionary, trying to work out not only the right wash cycle, but how to switch the machine on at all.

Or having a client who keeps saying 'Ne', which in my country means 'No', but in that particular country means 'Yes'.

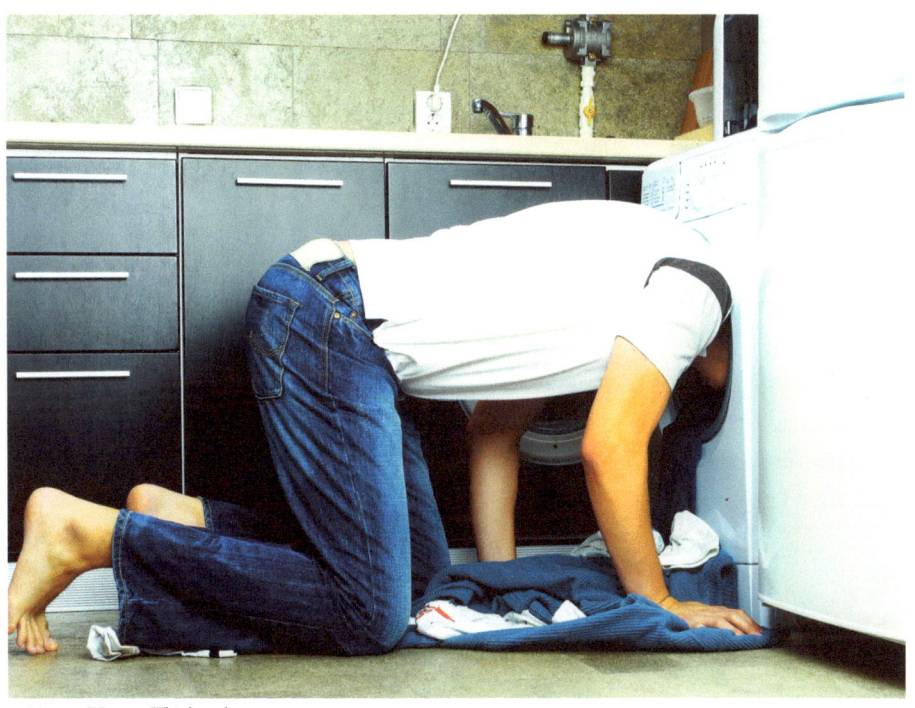

© Hemera/Hemera/Thinkstock

Coming back from abroad

I remember coming back to London after working abroad for a year and arriving at Waterloo Station with a feeling of great relief.

I sat with my daughter in one of the cafés and for the first time in my life, I couldn't care less about the weather, the healthcare, the education or the transport.

All I could think of was the humour, the eccentricity, a decent curry and being back in Soho.

Two months later, my enthusiasm still hadn't dampened, even though I still had no GP, I had been gazumped on the flat, and the only school that had space for my daughter was on the other side of town.

The curry was good, and I was back in Soho.

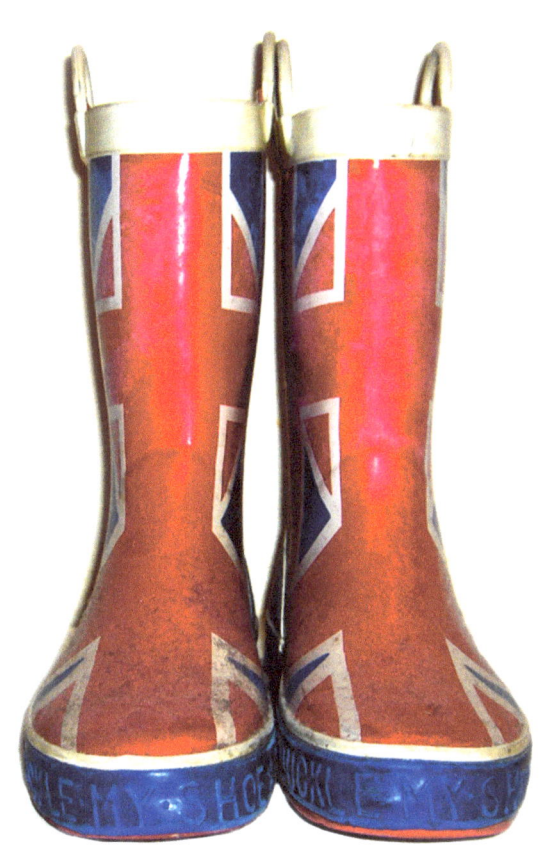

It's a boy's world

Most of the creative jobs in post-production are done by men.
And most of the support jobs are done by women.
That's nothing new.
A creative job requires long irregular hours and a fair amount of weekend work.
That's all very well until one decides to have a family. Then the man continues to work and the woman stays at home.
Of course, as always, there are exceptions to the rule.
I gave birth six weeks early, straight after my last day at work.
I was back five weeks later, so technically I was back before I had given birth.
Don't get me wrong. I wouldn't recommend this to anyone.

Too old to work, too young to die

If you are part of a senior workforce, you are 'out'.
Don't sound so surprised.
There are good reasons for this: you know too much, you are organised and you could do your job with your eyes closed.
So what is the problem?
You are tilting the balance of the boat filled with twenty-year-olds – 'in' ones who can't spell tlevision.
You see?
And you are unbalancing the balance sheets.
By the way, it's nothing personal.

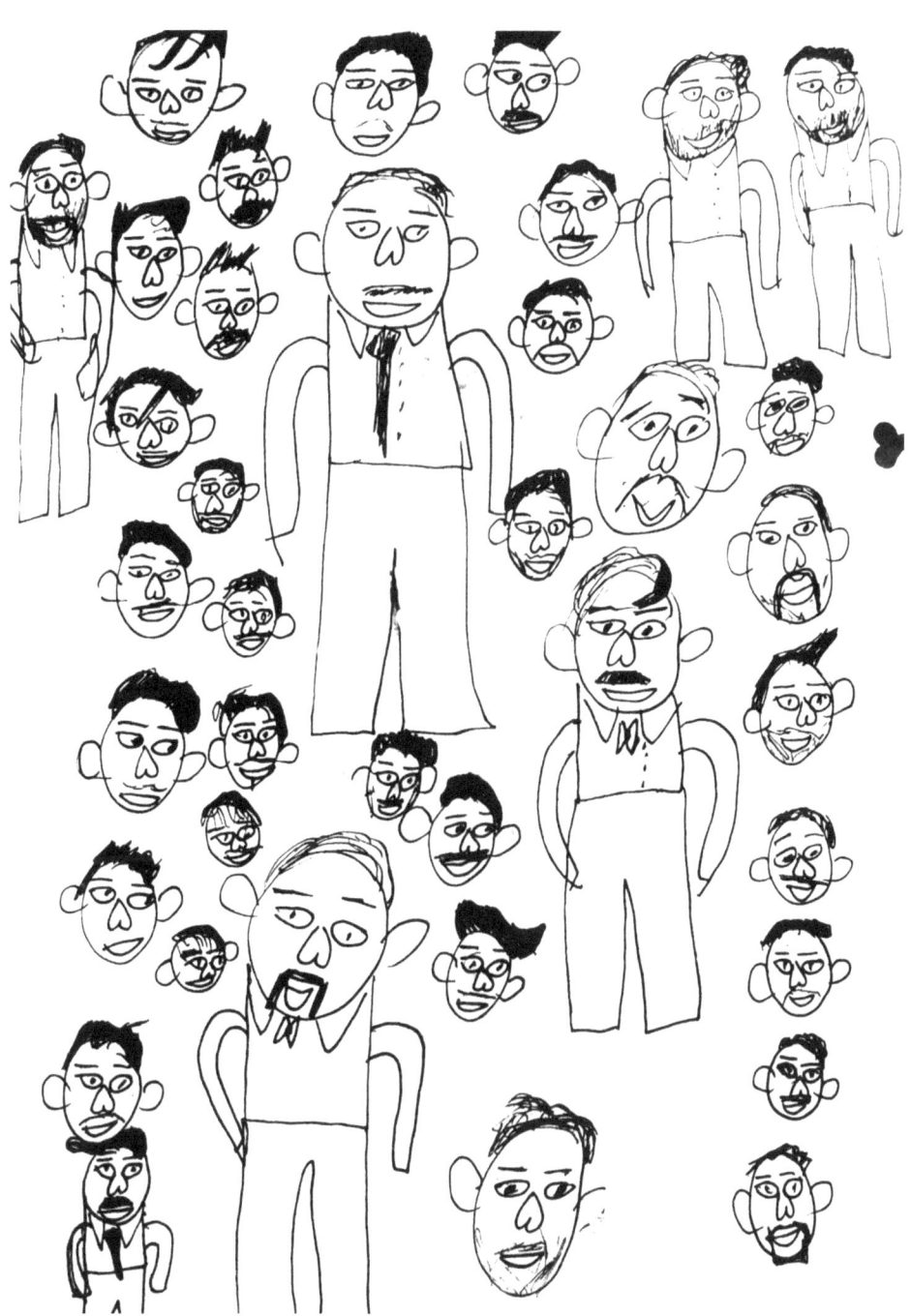

© Ivana Smokovic

Loyalty is out of the window

Sometime ago, you could be confident of getting the next job after completing the current one successfully as a company and as an individual.
'You are as good as your last job' is just another myth – now the spreadsheets rule. The profit margins have to keep rising.
The budgets keep shrinking.
Everybody is on the lookout for cheaper services and the companies are on the lookout for cheaper labour.
So loyalty is out of the equation.

Together you can say no

A lot of students ask me if they should join a union.
Remember: there's safety in numbers.
As an individual, you don't have the power to protect your rights.
As an individual, you have to say 'Yes'.
Only united are you able to say 'No'.
Don't forget: even companies merge to make themselves stronger.

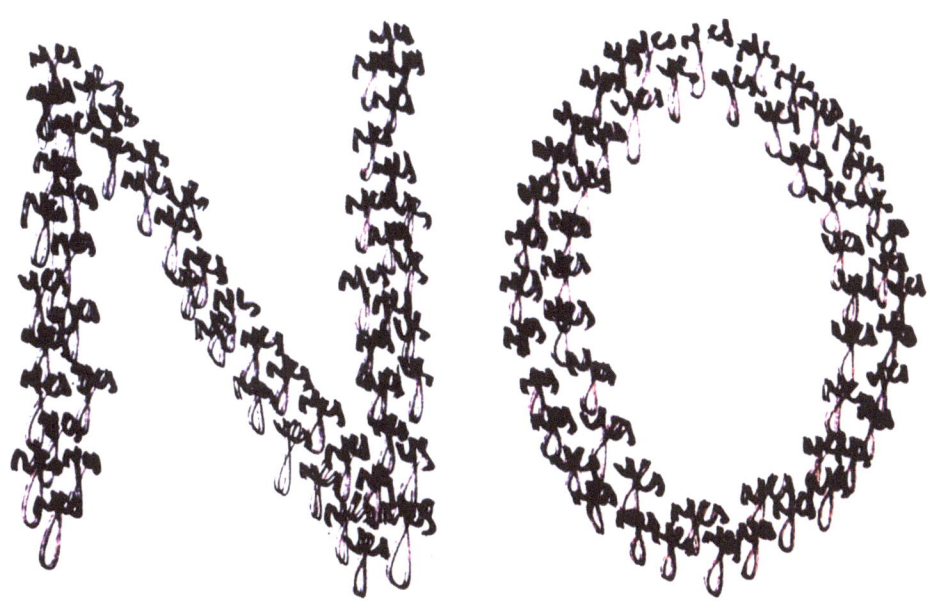

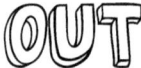

"When one door closes, another opens"
Alexander Graham Bell

A creative told me recently that students at his university are taught to expect to be made redundant on average five times during their career.

So don't be surprised when the department you work for closes suddenly and for no apparent reason.

Or if the company you work for unexpectedly (usually just before Christmas) announces a number of redundancies, even though it has made record profits.

1. Stay calm and focused.

2. Get legal advice.

3. Get the payout that will give you enough breathing space to pull yourself back together.

4. Get a good reference.

5. Get the next job.

Remember, you have to keep the industry moving:

onwards and upwards.

APPENDIX

Where are the jobs?

Post–production work has traditionally been created in post–production facilities that are able to look after the whole of the post–production. However, there are also a number of small facilities specialising in different segments of post-production. Over the last ten years, there has also been an increase in in-house post-production departments that are springing up in production companies and advertising agencies.

The majority of film visual effects work is still created in large post-production facilities that can expand and contract their workforce rapidly on a project-by-project basis.

Advertising post-production is still largely completed in the post-production facilities.

Television post-production may be done in-house or in a post-production facility. It all depends on the type of work and, of course, the budget.

Film, advertising or TV?

Post-production may follow a similar pipeline in film, television and advertising but there is a distinct difference between the three in the actual work, the work conditions, the work environment, the skills distribution and sometimes even the personality requirements.

Someone dynamic who thrives on constant change may find the pace of film frustrating and be more suited to advertising where turn-around is fairly quick and so the work more varied. However, the constant interaction with clients in advertising requires a highly communicative and outgoing personality.

A multitalented individual dabbling in 3D, 2D and motion graphics may find film and advertising too restrictive, with their more specialised and narrowly defined post-production roles and be more suited to TV, where multi talent is greatly appreciated.

I want to make ads

Who doesn't?

Advertising creates an infinitely nicer world than the one we live in. The world of singing blackcurrants, talking animals, dancing bank managers, wriggling salamis, friendly aliens and perfect, never ageing, beauties. In advertising the brands have to be polished and brought to perfection, even if it means making them perfectly ugly. Advertising is all about the image because good-looking brands sell and sales keep the shareholders happy.

Advertising clients sometimes spend more on their commercial, per one minute screen time, than a film studio does on a feature film, and some brands spend more on advertising and marketing than on the actual manufacture of their products. Smoothing out the skin of a model, removing the pips from fruit, adding the pips to fruit, filling the pies with more meat and removing the cork in a glass of wine are just some of the everyday requests in post-production.

The pressure of creating the perfect image that will sell the sometimes imperfect product raises the stress levels of everyone involved. That's why advertising post-production suites are the epitome of comfort, with chunky leather sofas, discreet lighting, computer games and a constant supply of food and drink. The clients walking into the suite have spent months - sometimes more than a year - in the development of the advert from the original idea through numerous rewrites, clients' feedback and research groups before they actually get to make it.

And now it has to be made perfect.

To succeed in advertising post-production, you have to be able to perform and stay calm under intense pressure.

You also have to have highly developed communication skills, as some clients want to chat, some don't. Some want you to be creative, some don't. Some will want you to express an opinion and some won't.

However, advertising post-production offers great remuneration for talented and creative people who thrive under pressure and take pride in creating beautiful and polished work.

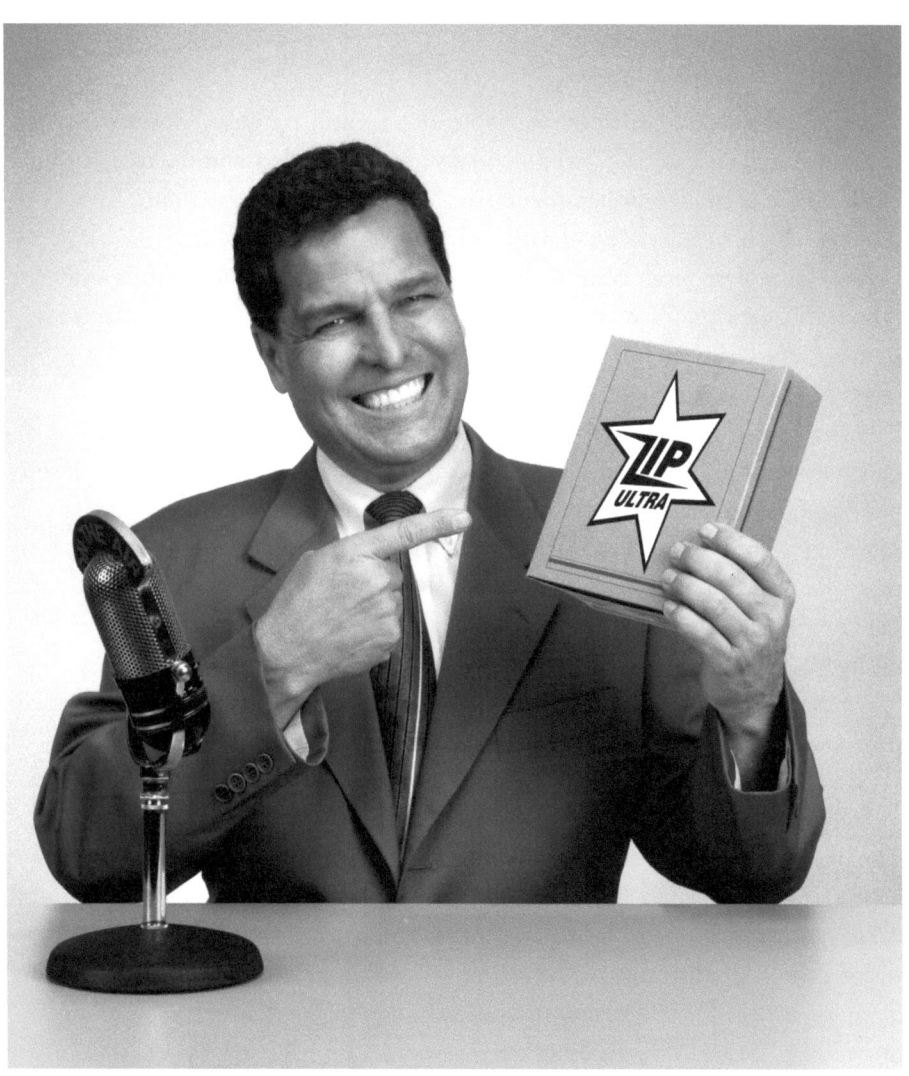

I want to make films

Then you don't belong with those people who are still arguing about poor scripts with no storylines and bad acting – those who don't understand the true purpose of film. Film is about entertainment. And, these days, good entertainment requires a lot of visual effects. That's great news!

Because, film post-production requires a constant supply of movie buffs with talent and a passion for visual effects. Film post-production is not, for the most part, a client-facing environment. Therefore, some of the perks enjoyed by advertising counterparts are omitted sorry, no sofas and no refreshments.

The good news is that so are some of the demands on one's personality. If you are good at what you do, especially in visual effects, you can be as introverted as you like, though you still have to be able to communicate with your colleagues at some level. Anyway, most of the time you will be surrounded by a few dozen people who are all listening to their ipods. Remember?

Due to greater and greater demand for visual effects not necessarily matched by greater and greater budgets the visual effects roles in film post-production are much more segmented and specialised in order to speed up the post-production process and deliver films to ever tighter deadlines.

This is very good news, as there are entry-level opportunities for those who have mastered some essential skills like rotoscoping or paint and rig removal.

The pre requisite for these roles would be the completion of a compositing course, combined with a good showreel.

A Hollywood action blockbuster may have thousands of visual effects shots of varied complexity that need to be completed within a six-month deadline. This is often impossible for one facility to undertake and in London, big projects are often shared between the facilities.

The remuneration in film post-production is not as high as in advertising but a credit on film will make you immortal. The work is project-based and on a freelance contract, renowned as 'feast or famine', because there are sometimes long gaps between the projects. The upside of working on feature film is that you gain immeasurable experience and knowledge, as you are surrounded by some of the greatest talent in post-production.

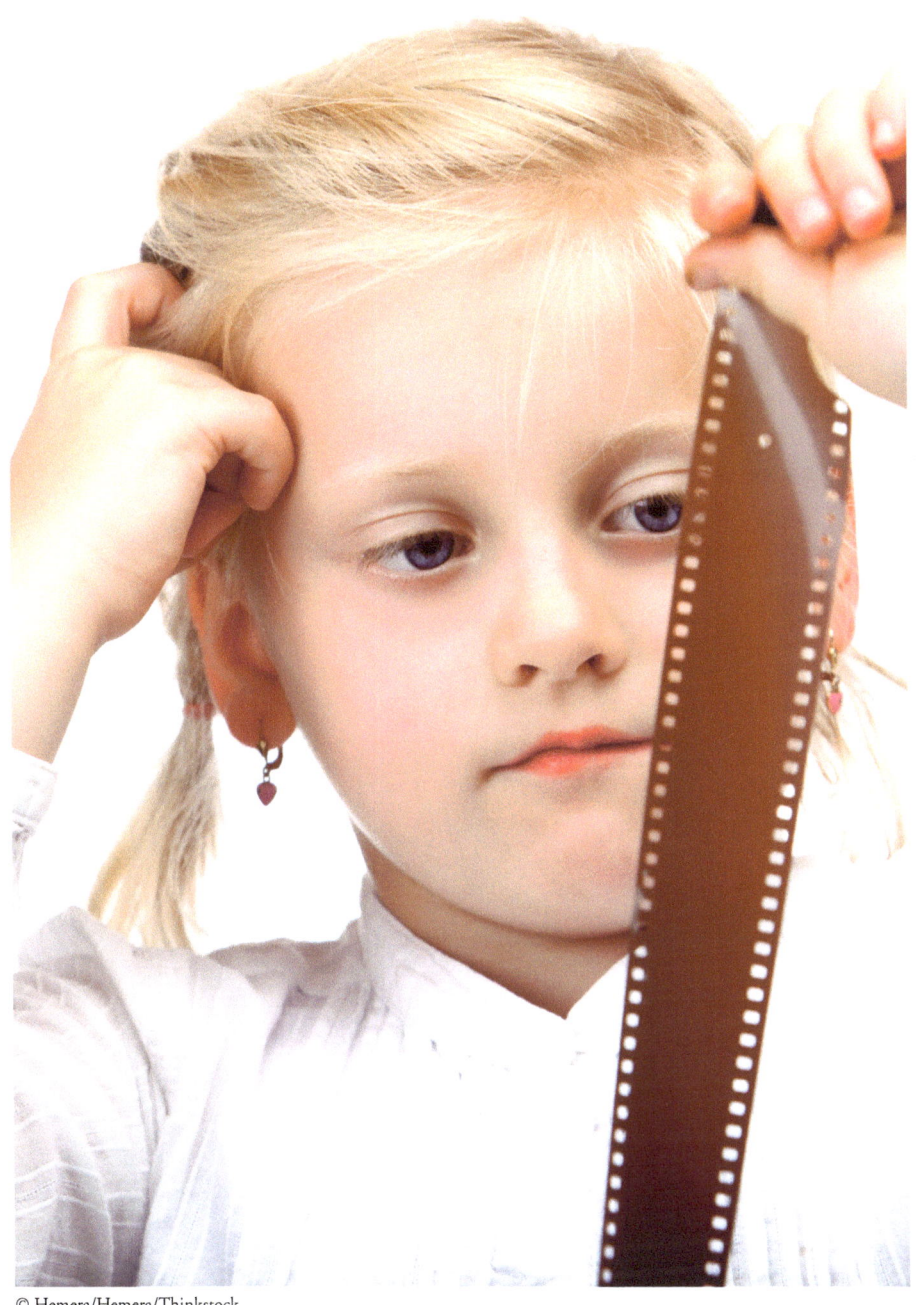
© Hemera/Hemera/Thinkstock

I want to make TV programmes

Then you don't mind that the documentaries have been pushed out to make way for reality shows and World cinema has been pushed out to make way for lifestyle programmes.

And the budgets have shrunk.

You are right, because great programmes are still being made. And you could contribute to making them even better.

Editing, grading, sound and motion graphics are constant requirements in TV but, increasingly, natural history documentaries, historical docu-dramas and dramas require visual effects too.

The other programmes that teach us how to cook, how to bring up children and how to dress all require title sequences, occasional graphics and TV promotions. For an ideas person there are great opportunities in television post-production and the appreciation of multi-talented individuals is greater than anywhere else. This is also because the budgets are smaller than in film and advertising.

Short-form work like title sequences, promotions, content graphics and idents can offer opportunities to be part of the whole process, from concept to delivery. The remuneration in TV post-production is lower than in film and advertising; however, opportunities for creative freedom often compensate for that.

The working environment varies but it's often quite relaxed and informal filled with chatty and interesting people.

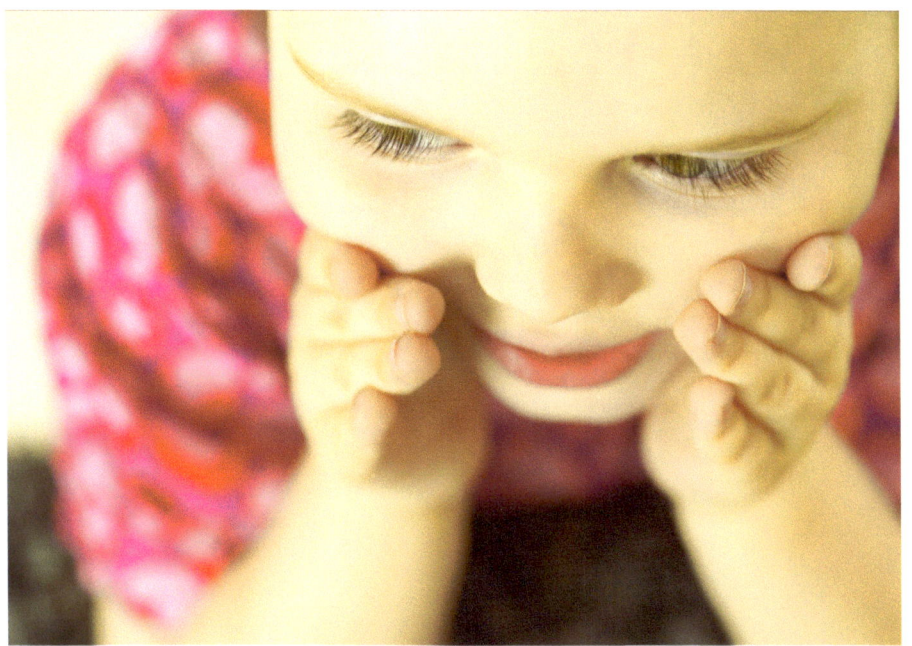

© Getty Images/Photos.com/Thinkstock

SKILLS MATCHED TO JOBS

I love people

You could be the man in the middle: a post-production producer.

To be the man in the middle, one needs excellent communication skills due to constant interaction with the clients – who need constant attention – and the artists – who need constant mothering.

So you need to be a good listener and a social animal.

You also need a high level of emotional intelligence and diplomacy, as you are dealing with a very wide range of personalities and some very big egos.

The post-production producer is responsible for the smooth flow of post-production and delivery of the job to the client's specification and on schedule. However, jobs rarely run smoothly so the ability to think on one's feet and stay calm under pressure are the pre-requisites for this job.

Other tasks involve preparing cost estimates and sourcing relevant production elements from the client like artwork, logos and music.

Knowledge of post-production and having an excellent eye for detail are essential, as are organisational and managerial skills.

I love colouring

But do you know enough, or are you at least willing to learn about
cinematography, the cameras, the lenses and the film stock?

The telecine artist (colourist/grader) transfers film to tape or digital disk, if shot
on film, and grades it by adjusting the colours on individual shots to ensure
colour consistency throughout the film.

He balances the colours of the shots that have been filmed under different
weather and lighting conditions, at different times of day or on different
locations. He is expected to have a creative input into fixing problems like over-
exposure or under-exposure, colour casts and anything else that may affect the
consistency of the film grade. Often different parts of the picture, like skin tones
or skies, need to be isolated to treat them separately.

In advertising, the advertised product and logos are usually isolated and treated
differently from the rest of the film, as they have to retain the true colours of the
branding.

It sounds fun, but this is also a highly-skilled job that is enormously respected in
the industry and some telecine artists become almost 'stars' because of their
grading skills. They often become renowned for, and associated with, a particular
look they give to films. I never fail to spot one grading artist's work and am very
pleased with myself when his name scrolls up on the credits at the end of the TV
programme.

As a telecine artist works closely with the director and the director of
photography, he also requires great communication skills and the ability to work
under pressure.

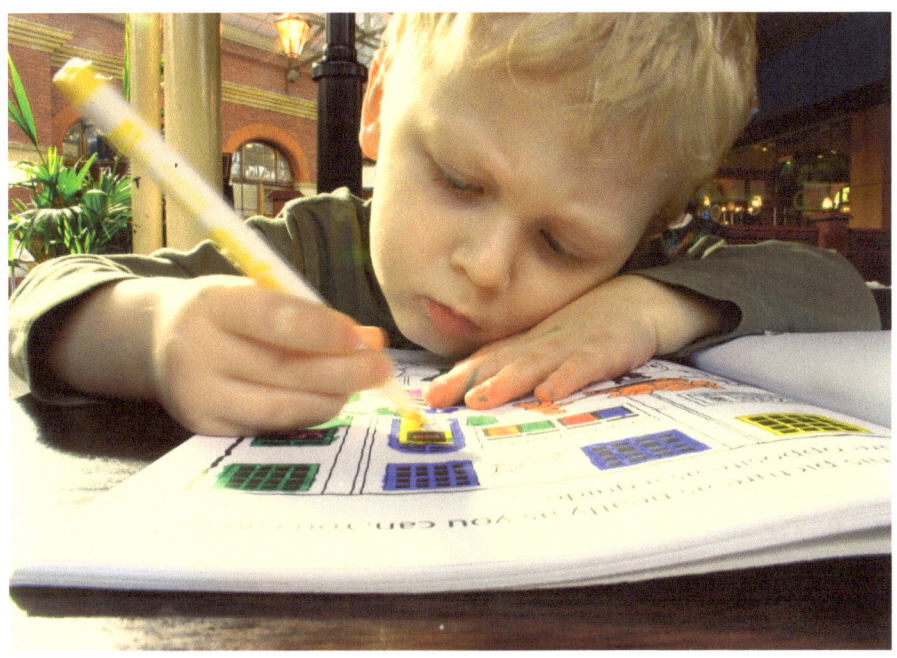
© iStockphoto/iStockphoto/Thinkstock

I love stories

If you love reading and telling stories you may want to become an editor.
The editor cuts and assembles raw filmed material, adding graphics, audio and any other elements to create a flowing, coherent whole. He may be required to create some of the placeholder elements, graphics or effects that will be replaced by final elements at a later stage. This is a highly creative role, as the actors' performance, the dialogue, the pace, the images and the music all have to be taken into consideration and combined to fulfil the director's brief and to achieve his vision.

The editor creates an edited film – an offline – from low-resolution footage (to save disk space), which, when approved, is conformed (reassembled) i.e. replaced by full resolution graded footage via the edit decision list. This is usually done by an online editor. Final graphics, animations, visual effects, titles and audio are then added.

The editors are often given a lot of creative freedom in the creation of a film, an advert or a TV programme.

They have to be great storytellers and be able to create the right timing, tension and flow of the film. A great attention to detail, the ability to work under pressure, organisational and communication skills are a must.

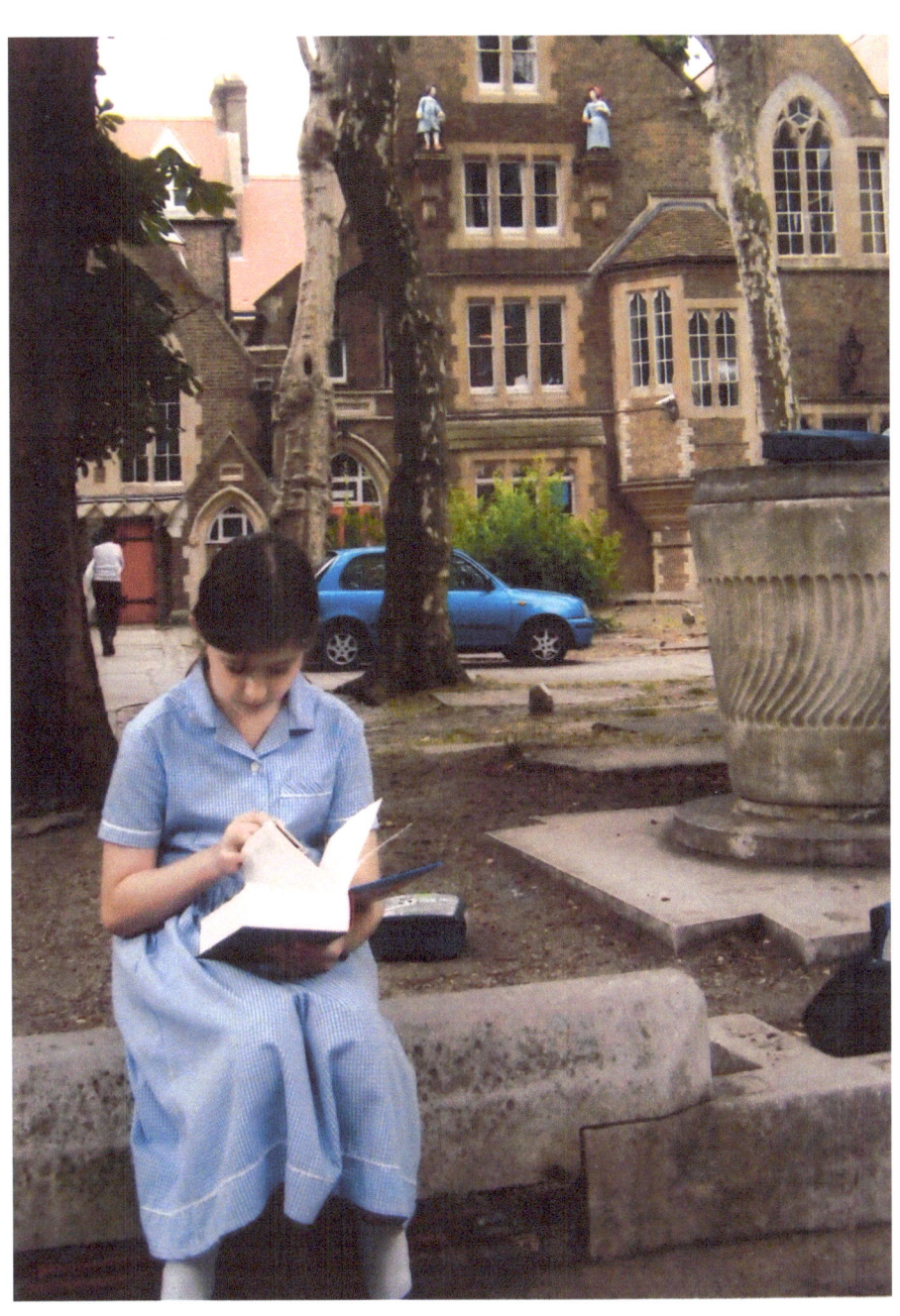

I love magic

The visual effects supervisor is in charge of magic.

Shots that cannot be captured in one pass by the camera fall under visual effects. Visual effects shots are made of multiple elements - at least two – that have been either shot separately or are to be combined at a later stage with computer-generated elements, or both.

Sometimes more than a hundred different elements are combined to create the final shot. While the perception of visual effects is still Star Wars imagery, visual effects are mostly used to create photorealistic shots.

The visual effects supervisor is involved in the project from the pre-production stage, when all the aspects of the shoot are planned, and he suggests the most efficient ways of solving complex sequences that are impossible, impractical, too expensive or too dangerous to shoot in camera in one pass.

The visual effects supervisor attends the shoot and sometimes directs the second unit, filming the elements like dust or explosions to be used in post-production. He then oversees the visual effects post-production.

An eye for detail, a deep understanding of both production and post-production techniques and good communication and organisational skills are essential. An understanding of technical on-set equipment like cameras, film stock and lights, as well as post-production software, is critical.

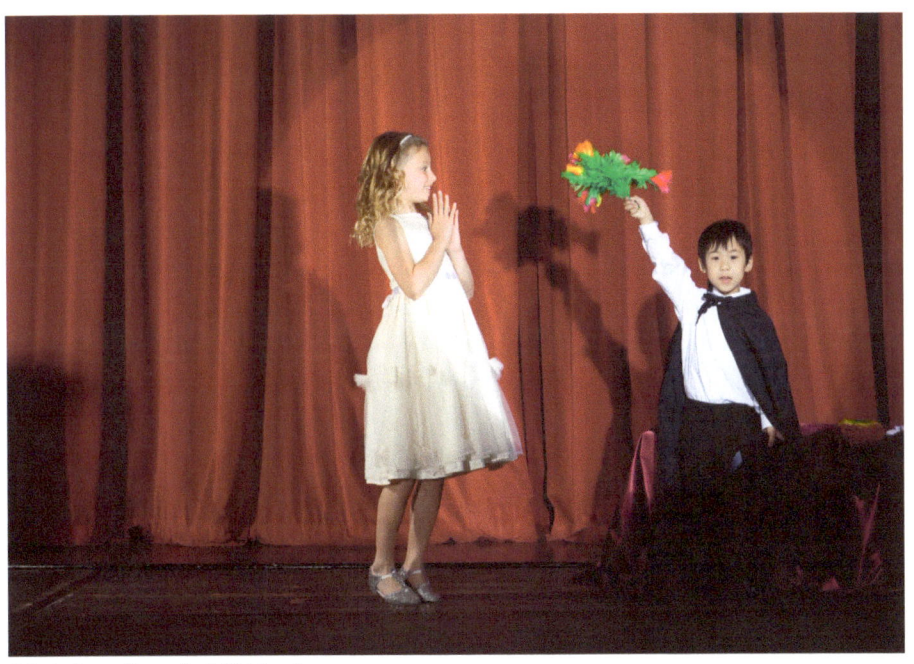

© Jupiterimages/BananaStock/Thinkstock

I love building things

But want to keep your hands clean?

You could be a 3D (CG) visual effects artist who creates computer-generated 3D objects, creatures and sets that are either stills or animated. If CG elements are to be combined with live action, the 3D artist tracks live action movement, using a process known as match-moving, creating a 3D camera that emulates the movement of the live action one. This camera is then used to place CG elements into the live action shot. The 3D artist also creates textures that will be mapped onto CG elements, generates particles for elements like rain or snow and lights the scene.

In film post-production, the 3D artist's role is much more specialised and is split into a number of roles like modeller, animator, lighting TD, rigger, match-mover, render wrangler and so on, while in advertising and TV short-form projects, more generalised (3D generalist) skills are often required.

The core skills of the 3D artist are a deep understanding of animation, maths and physics. Attention to detail, patience, the ability to work under pressure, the ability to take criticism and to keep up with the schedule are a must.

Good communication skills are a real asset.

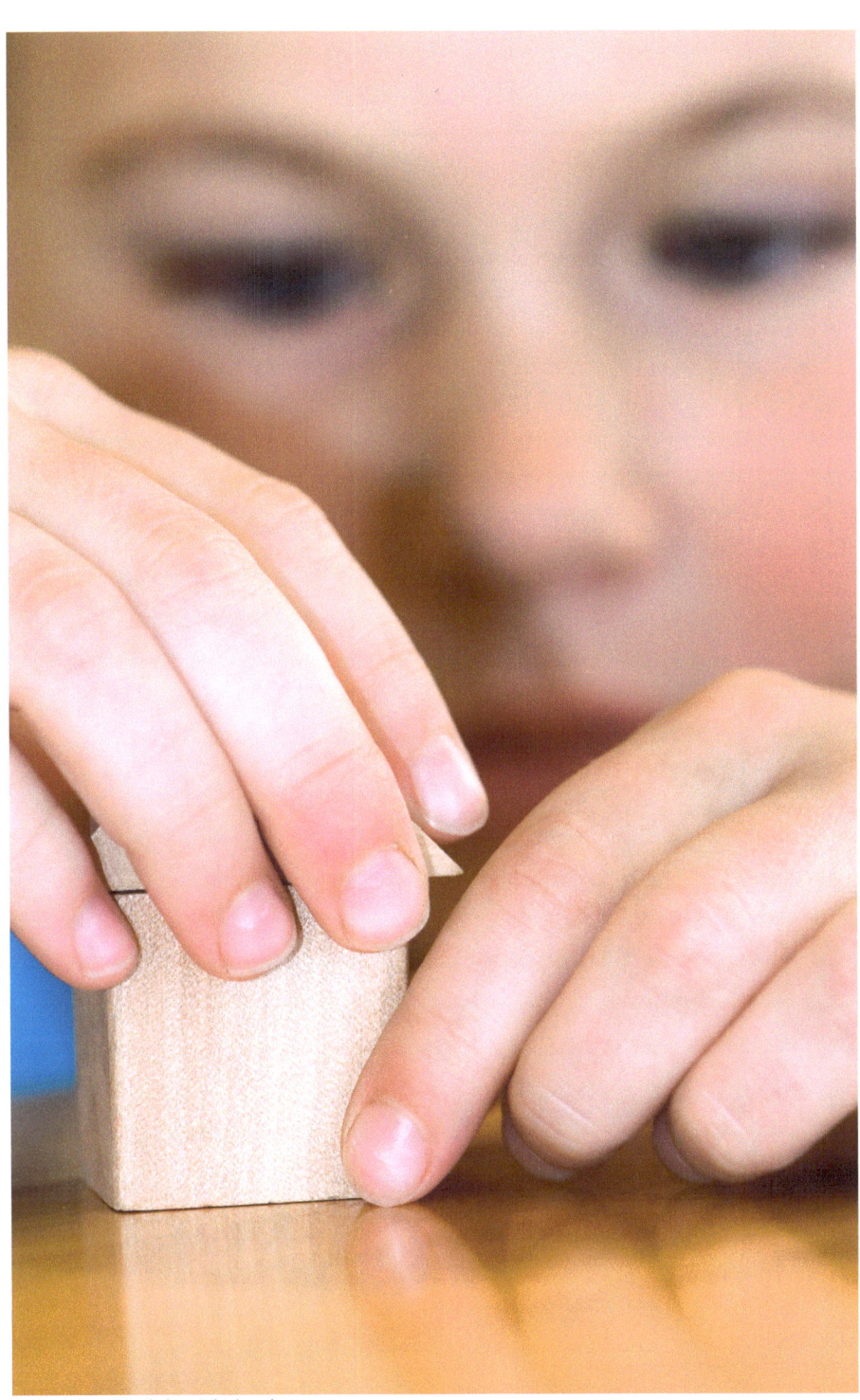

I love hiding things

Compositing is all about hiding things.

The 2D (compositor) visual effects artist uses separate elements to create a final shot by either combining live action plates shot in different locations or by combining live action plates with CG elements and/or graphics ones.

There may be hundreds of different elements that need to be combined together by either rotoscoping (cutting out actors or foreground elements, sometimes frame by frame), keying (cutting out elements filmed on green/blue screen) or isolating elements by using pre-generated mattes from 3D.

Other common tasks are: rig removal (removing wires the actors are suspended on or various rigs), removing tracking markers that have been placed on the live action plates for the ease of tracking, tracking (emulating the movement of the background to drop in foreground elements), retouching, adding additional effects like mist, dust, explosions and so on.

Different elements need to be colour- corrected when combined to create an illusion that they were shot for real in one camera pass.

The core skills are the same as the 3D artist's skills, though maths and physics are, thankfully, not essential. An understanding of colour, lighting and composition are crucial, as is the ability to take direction and having good communication skills.

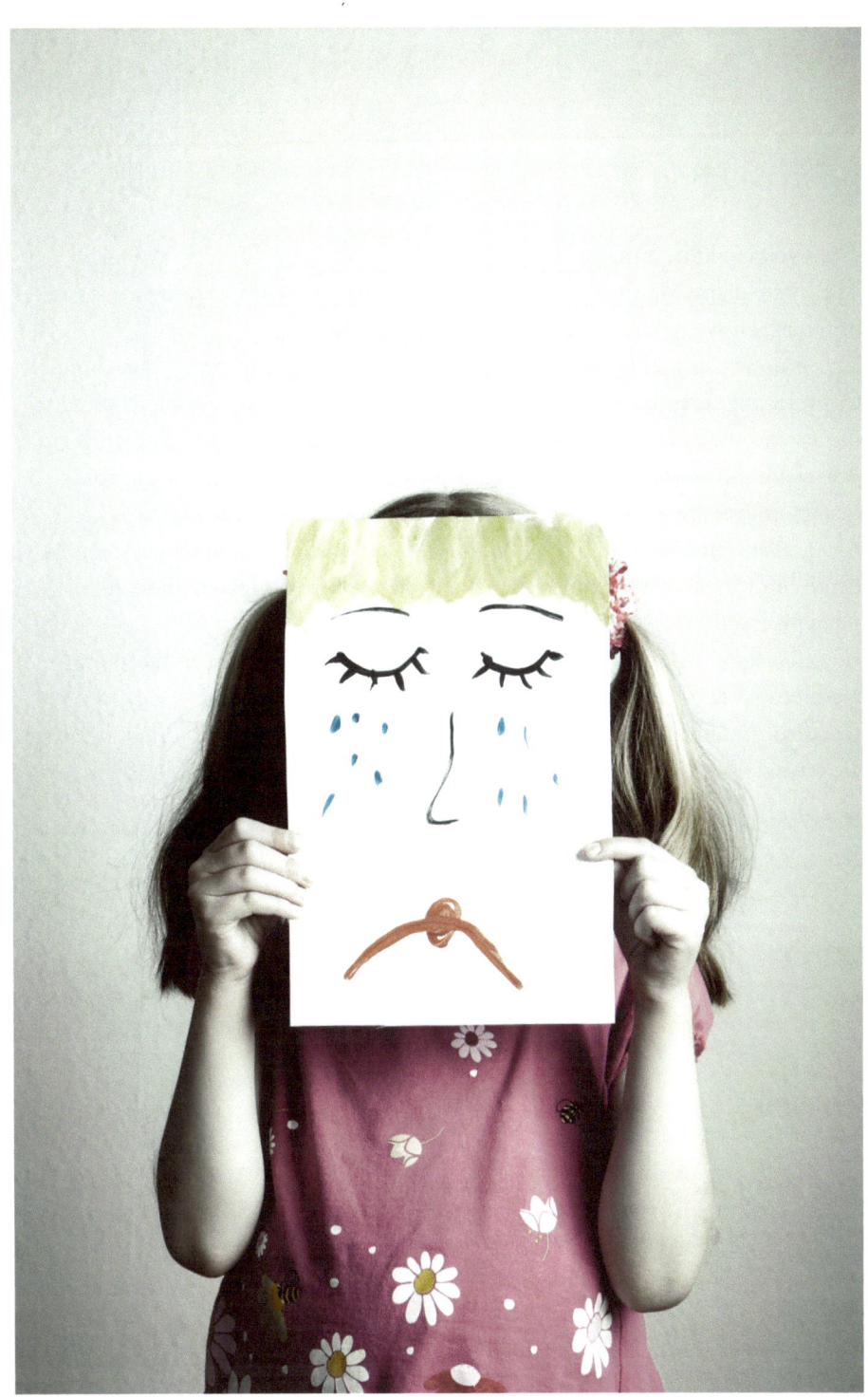

I love painting

Then you could be a matte painter.

The matte painter creates photorealistic environments when they are impossible or too expensive to shoot, or when they simply don't exist.

This is done using 2D paint techniques and, increasingly, using 2.5D techniques by projecting textures onto geometry. Sometimes, matte painters are required to just extend the environment or embellish the existing one.

A background in fine art, combined with a passion for creating photographic quality images are a must, as is the knowledge of Photoshop.

An excellent understanding of photography, composition, camera focal lengths, depth of field, shadows, light and perspective, and a vivid imagination are prerequisites for developing into a successful matte painter.

An understanding and some basic knowledge of 3D software is an increasing requirement due to a close working relationship with 3D.

Good communication skills and the ability to take direction and, often, criticism, are crucial.

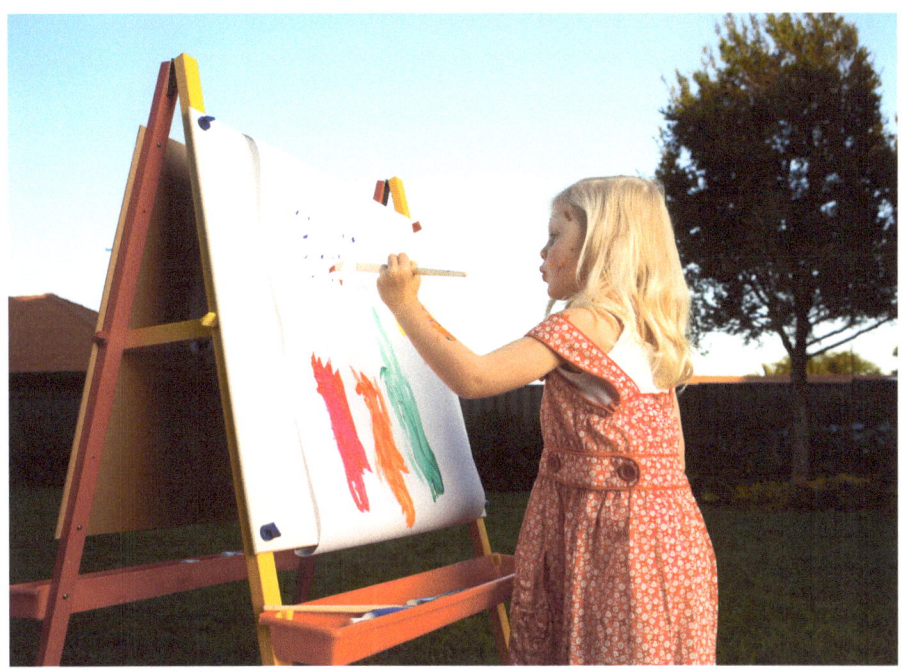

© Steve Baccon/Photodisc/Thinkstock

I love motion graphics

The motion graphics artist designs and animates graphic elements, including typography, and combines them with CG and/or live action.

Even though motion graphics falls into the realm of 2D, motion graphics artists often use 3D software too, which enables them to create 3D logos and other 3D elements to be combined with graphics generated in 2D software.

Particle animation is a key element of motion graphics that is often used to implode or explode logos or to create elements like fog or smoke.

Motion graphics are used across the industry from title sequences and idents to animation or manipulation of brand logos and names.

This is a very creative role that often requires coming up with the concept, executing it and delivering it for, increasingly, a variety of mediums.

A background in graphic design and the ability to communicate a creative idea are crucial.

A passion for editing and motion graphics, combined with creativity, attention to detail, the ability to work under pressure and having great interpersonal skills are a must.

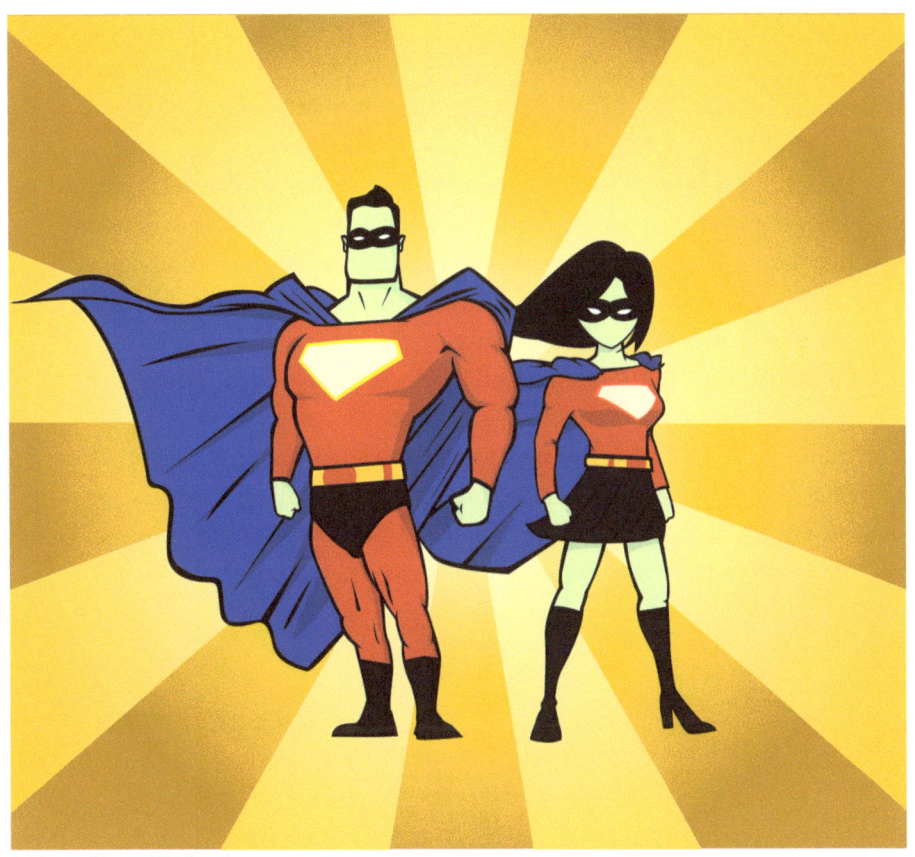

© Hemera/Hemera/Thinkstock

I love music

If listening to music is not enough and you are not that good at composing music, you could be a sound editor.

The sound editor creates the soundtrack by combining separate elements of voiceover, sound effects, dialogue and music. The elements are edited, balanced, mixed and synchronised to the picture to create a final master audio.

This is a highly creative role, as sound makes a great difference to the perception of moving images. It plays with our emotions by enhancing the dramatic elements of the film, often foreshadowing the change in mood. This is usually done in a very subtle way that we are often not even aware of.

The sound designer works closely with the director and a composer and often contributes suggestions and ideas, so communication skills are a must.

Having a good ear, a good sense of timing and a deep knowledge of music, sound and the sound industry are essential - as is a technical knowledge of sound equipment.

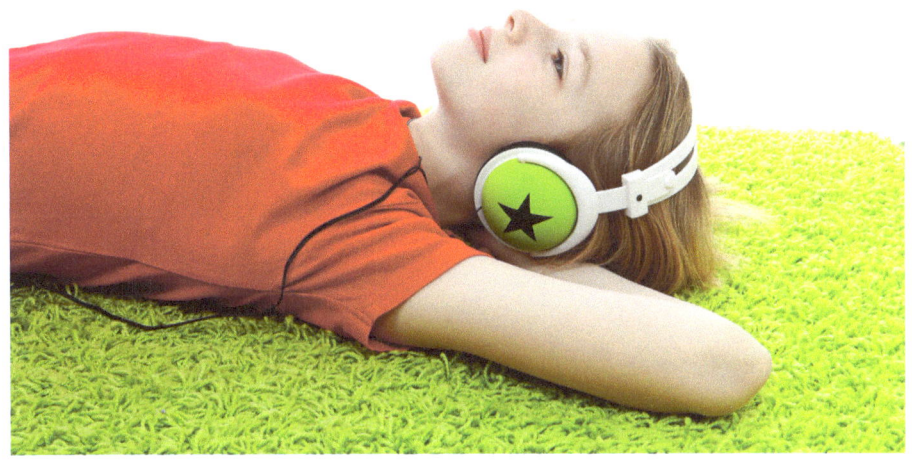
© iStockphoto/iStockphoto/Thinkstock

THE CLIENTS

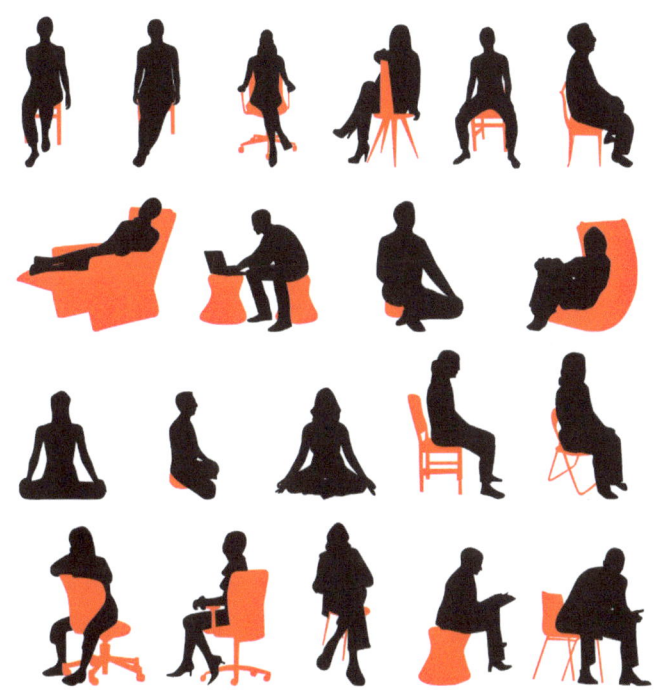

Who is who in advertising?

In advertising post-production there are a number of clients beside the actual client whose brand is being advertised: the advertising agency that came up with a concept and the commercials production company, assigned by the advertising agency to shoot the advert.

The brand's client will most often come with another person from the company, the advertising agency will be represented by the creatives (a copywriter and an art director), the account manager, the agency TV producer and at least one production assistant. The production company will be represented by, at least, the commercial's director and the commercial's producer.

Who does what in advertising?

The **commercial client** is a marketing manager for the brand, the government organisation or the charity that is being advertised. He has the ultimate control.
The **advertising agency creatives** come up with the idea for the commercial and select a commercials director to film it.
The **advertising agency account manager** is the key advertising agency contact with the client.
The **advertising agency TV producer** holds the purse strings for the production and post-production and is the key link between the agency, the production company and the post-production facility.
The **commercial's producer** is responsible for the smooth production of the shoot. The **commercial's director** contributes his ideas to and develops the creatives' concept, directs the shoot and oversees the post-production.

Who is who in film?

In film post-production, the main clients are the film producer, the film director and the director of photography (DOP). If you are a visual effects artist, your client will most likely be the film visual effects supervisor and sadly – or sometimes luckily – you may never meet the film's director, the producer or the DOP.

Who does what in film?

The **film producer** develops the project, raises the finance and looks after the logistics of the whole production, hiring key staff.

The **film director** is the creative force of the film. He directs the actors and the crew on the shoot and oversees all the creative aspects of the creation of the film.

The **director of photography** (DOP) is responsible for the visual look of the film through lighting, framing and camera moves.

Who is who in TV?

In television post-production the clients are the TV programme director and the TV programme producer (though these roles are sometimes combined into one), and the commissioning editor.

Who does what in TV?

The **TV programme producer** pitches the project to the commissioning editor and looks after the logistics of the whole production, including finance and administration.

The **TV programme director** is involved in the creative aspects of making the programme, directs the shoot and oversees the post-production.

The **commissioning editor** chooses programme ideas for the TV broadcaster he is employed by, that production companies have pitched to him. He then allocates budgets to the production companies to create programmes from the selected ideas. He has the ultimate creative control in the making of the TV programme.

USEFUL INFORMATION

Networking and showreel websites

Facebook – *friends' networking site* www.facebook.com
Flickr – *photos sharing* www.flickr.com
LinkedIn – *professional networking site* www.linkedin.com
Myspace – *friends networking site* www.mspace.com
Vimeo – *videos and showreels* www.vimeo.com
YouTube – *videos and showreels* www.youtube.com

Selection of UK organisations and associations

BKSTS – the moving image society
www.bksts.com
British Film Institute – leading body for film in the UK
www.bfi.org.uk
Film London – London film and media agency
www.filmlondon.org.uk
IPS – Institute of Professional Sound
www.ips.org.uk
IVCA – International Visual Communications Association
www.ivca.org
PACT – Producers Alliance for Cinema and Television
www.pact.co.uk
RTS – The Royal Television Society
www.rts.org.uk
Skillset – industry body offering advice, resources and training
www.skillset.org
UK Screen Association – trade body representing UK post-production industry
www.ukscreenassociation.co.uk
Women in Film and Television – women's voice in creative media
www.wftv.org.uk

Comprehensive listings of UK courses

Hotcourses – listing of short, undergraduate and postgraduate courses
www.hotcourses.com
UCAS – listing of university and college courses
www.ucas.com

Selection of UK post-production colleges and schools

BBC Academy – face-to-face and online courses
www.bbcacademy.com
Bournemouth University – short, undergraduate and postgraduate courses
www.bournemouth.ac.uk
Escape Studios – specialist VFX classroom or online short courses
www.escapestudios.co.uk
Met Film School – short, undergraduate and postgraduate courses
www.metfilmschool.co.uk
National Film and Television School – short diploma and MA courses
www.nftsfilm-tv.ac.uk
Raindance – independent filmmaking short courses
www.raindance.co.uk
Ravensbourne College – short, undergraduate and postgraduate courses
www.rave.ac.uk
Soho Editors – short software courses for media professionals
www.sohoeditors.com

Online courses

Animation A-Team – visual effects creature animation school
www.animationateam.com
Class On Demand – production and post-production
trainingwww.classondemand.net
cmi-VFX – visual effects training
www.cmivfx.com
Digital Tutors – visual effects and animation tutorials
www.digitaltutors.com
The Foundry – compositing tutorials for Nuke and their other products
www.thefoundry.co.uk
fxphd – visual effects and production training
www.fxphd.com
Gnomon – visual effects school
www.gnomonschool.com
Steve Wright Digital Effects – compositing school from compositing guru
www.swdfx.com
Video Copilot – after effects tutorials
www.videocopilot.net

Selection of hardware and software manufacturers

Adobe
www.adobe.com

Apple
www.apple.com

Autodesk
www.autodesk.co.uk

Avid
www.avid.com

Blackmagic Design
www.blackmagic-design.com

Digital Film Technology
www.dft-film.com

eyeon Software
www.eyeonline.com

The Foundry
www.thefoundry.co.uk

New Tek
www.newtek.com

Quantel
www.quantel.com

Comprehensive listings of companies and crews

The Knowledge – UK and international production suppliers including post-production facilities
www.theknowledgeonline.com

 The Broadcast Production Guide – suppliers and service providers within the broadcasting sector
www.theproductionguide.co.uk

Jobs and industry magazines

Brand Republic – advertising, marketing, media and PR news and jobs
www.brandrepublic.com
Broadcast Freelancer – freelance jobs in TV and Radio
www.broadcastfreelancer.com
Broadcast – TV and radio industry news, data and analysis
www.broadcastnow.co.uk
Chinwag – new media news and jobs
www.chinwag.com
Campaign – advertising news and jobs
www.campaignlive.co.uk
Computer Arts – news, reviews and tips on digital art
www.computerarts.co.uk
Creative Pool – creative recruitment and directory resource
www.creativepool.co.uk
Creative Review – visual communications magazine, news and jobs
www.creativereview.co.uk
Design Week – design news and jobs
www.designweek.co.uk
Digital Arts – inspiration for digital creatives
www.digitalartsonline.co.uk
4 Regional Film and Video – regional film and video news and jobs
www.4rfv.co.uk
fx-guide – VFX guide, tips and training
www.fxguide.com
grapevine jobs – jobs in entertainment and media
www.grapevinejobs.co.uk
The Guardian – media news and jobs
www.guardian.co.uk
Mandy – film and broadcast resource and jobs
www.mandy.com
Media UK – news, directory and jobs in radio and the press

www.mediauk.com

Media Week – media news, directories and jobs
www.mediaweek.com

ProductionBase – film, television and commercials jobs
www.productionbase.co.uk

shots – showcase, news and directory of creative media
www.shots.net

Televisual – broadcast and production magazine
www.televisual.com

The Stage – entertainment industry news, how to guides and jobs
www.thestage.co.uk

3D Total – 3d artist's forum and jobs
www.3dtotal.com

Variety – film news, awards, festivals and jobs (USA)
www.variety.com

VFX Pro – VFX community and jobs
www.vfxpro.com

VFXrecruit – jobs in VFX, TV, games and film
www.vfx-recruit.com

Workstation – creative studio jobs
www.workstation.co.uk

The Trade Union

BECTU – The Media and Entertainment Union
www.bectu.org.uk

A selection of books to get you going

Acting for Animators, Ed Hooks: Routledge, 2011.

Animals in Motion, Eadweard Muybridge: Dover Publications, 1957. The *Animator's Survival Kit*, Richard E. Williams: Faber and Faber Ltd, 2009.

Audio Post Production for Television and Film: An Introduction to Technology and Techniques, Hilary Wyatt and Tim Amyes: Focal Press, 2004.

BBC VFX: The Story of the BBC Visual Effects Department, Mat Irvine and Mike Tucker: Aurum Press Ltd, 2010.

Cinematic Storytelling: The 100 Most Powerful Film Conventions Every Filmmaker Must Know, Jennifer Van Sijll: Michael Wiese Productions, 2005.

Color Correction for Video: Using Desktop Tools to Perfect Your Image (DV Expert Series), Steve Hullfish and Jaime Fowler: Focal Press, 2008.

Compositing Visual Effects: Essentials for the Aspiring Artist, Steve Wright: Focal Press, 2008.

Digital Compositing for Film and Video, Steve Wright: Focal Press, 2010.

Digital Lighting and Rendering, Jeremy Birn: New Riders, 2006.

Digital Texturing and Painting, Owen Demers: New Riders, 2001.

Film Editing: Great Cuts Every Filmmaker and Movie Lover Must Know, Gael Chandler: Michael Wiese Productions, 2009.

Fix It In Post: Solutions for Postproduction Problems, Jack James: Focal Press, 2009.

The Human Figure in Motion, Eadweard Muybridge: Dover Publications, 1955.

The Illusion of Life: Disney Animation, Frank Thomas and Ollie Johnston: Hyperion, 1997.

In the Blink of an Eye: A Perspective on Film Editing, Walter Murch: Silman-James Press, 2001.

Sound Design: The Expressive Power of Music, Voice and Sound Effects in Cinema, David Sonnenschein: Michael Wiese Productions, 2001.

The Sound Effects Bible: How to Create and Record Hollywood Style Sound Effects, Ric Viers: Michael Wiese Productions, 2008.

Timing for Animation, Harold Whitaker, John Halas and Tom Sito: Focal Press, 2009.

The Technique of Special Effects Cinematography, Raymond Fielding: Focal Press, 1985.

The Visual Effects Producer: Understanding the Art and Business of VFX, Charles Finance and Susan Zwerman: Focal Press, 2009.

The VES Handbook of Visual Effects: Industry Standard VFX Practices and Procedures, Jeffrey A. Okun and Susan Zwerman: Focal Press, 2010.

Video Editing and Post Production: A Professional Guide, Gary H Anderson: Focal Press, 1998.

Visual Effects for Film and Television, Mitch Mitchell: Focal Press, 2004.

Visual Effects in A Digital World: A Comprehensive Glossary of Over 7,000 Visual Effects Terms, Karen E. Goulekas: Morgan Kaufmann Publishers, 2001.

Thank you

Rosa Lykiardopoulos for the amazing cover. I love it!
www.insolentcandyfloss.com

Greg Loftin for his wise and detailed feedback after patiently reading my unedited book.

Mitch Mitchell for his incredibly humorous comments after also patiently reading my unedited book.

Charlie Wilson who bravely edited my book.

John Amy for graciously typesetting and designing the book.
www.promo-design.co.uk

Ted Hayton without whom I would never have entered the industry. I am thanking you!

Nadja and Jelena for their inspiration, endless support and encouragement.

My mother Majda for believing in this book, and for everything she taught me.

My daughter Ivana for her sharp and witty comments, and for putting up with burnt dinners.

Notes

www.ingramcontent.com/pod-product-compliance
Lightning Source LLC
Chambersburg PA
CBHW042348200526
45159CB00034BA/28